Straight Outta Crawley

www.penguin.co.uk

For more information on Romesh Ranganathan,
see his website at www.romeshranganathan.co.uk

Straight Outta Crawley

Memoirs of a Distinctly Average
Human Being

ROMESH RANGANATHAN

BANTAM PRESS

LONDON · NEW YORK · TORONTO · SYDNEY · AUCKLAND

TRANSWORLD PUBLISHERS
61–63 Uxbridge Road, London W5 5SA
www.penguin.co.uk

Transworld is part of the Penguin Random House group of companies
whose addresses can be found at global.penguinrandomhouse.com

First published in Great Britain in 2018 by Bantam Press
an imprint of Transworld Publishers

A CIP catalogue record for this book is available from the British Library.

ISBNS
9780593078259 (hc)
9780593078242 (tpb)

Typeset in 13.5/16 pt Garamond MT Std by Jouve (UK), Milton Keynes
Printed and bound in Great Britain by Clays Ltd, Elcograf S.p.A.

Penguin Random House is committed to a sustainable
future for our business, our readers and our planet. This book
is made from Forest Stewardship Council® certified paper.

MIX
Paper from
responsible sources
FSC
www.fsc.org   FSC® C018179

3 5 7 9 10 8 6 4 2

To Leesa and our beautiful children. I would not have
been able to do this without your ongoing ability to
generate such an intense financial pressure that
I feel I have to continue working. Love you.

Contents

Live from Bedford Stuyvesant: The Livest One

The title of this introduction is one of the best opening lines of all time. (It's mostly in the delivery.) It's from a song called 'Unbelievable' by the Notorious B.I.G., and I really want the opening of this book to be as good an introduction to me as that line is to him. But it's hard. Writing this book has been as challenging as trying to find a metaphor about what writing a book is like. At first, I really was convinced it was a great idea. I thought I could write about stuff that hadn't appeared in shows, or that I hadn't talked about in stand-up: it would give people an insight above and beyond – you'd get to see the real me, guys.

When it came to it, though, it quickly became clear that writing a book is no picnic.

It's very tricky to ascertain what's worthy of inclusion. Do you tell every story, or only the ones you'd tell down the pub? If someone is a national treasure, every single detail of their life is interesting. If you were reading a book by Stephen Fry, he'd say something like 'Well, you can imagine the confusion when I sat down to drink the tea, and they'd actually given me coffee!' You'd read that and tell your friends what a delight Stephen Fry is, and how down to earth he seems to be. I'm not at that level. I'm not even close to being a national treasure. I don't think you get national treasure status from coming runner-up in the Amused Moose new act competition. But if I was, I would just pack this book full of tea anecdotes and not bloody worry about it.

There's also part of me that wonders how you, the reader, have ended up holding this book. There's a good chance you've been given it as a present, so you may feel you have to read it because the giver may ask what you thought of it. I don't agree with that. I think if you're going to give someone a present and later ask for a review, you've given them a responsibility. You've given them the gift of pressure. But if you've bought it for yourself, thank you for helping me with my self-esteem issues.

It was my birthday recently and my mum bought me a suit. Before we get into this suit story, I should probably point out that I tend to go off at tangents. If you're not a tangent person, then put this down. This is not a book for you. If you've already bought the book, then I guess you'll have to bear with me. But if it's not your thing and you don't read to the end, I won't judge you and your questionable taste. I've started and abandoned so many books that I actually wondered if I might get away with writing half a book, then repeating it for the second half. I guess you'll just have to read on to see how that went.

My mum chose the suit and said she bought me what she thought I'd like. It's unusual to get a present that confirms your mother thinks you're a prick. The suit is rank. I haven't told her any of this, so it will be a good test of whether she actually reads this book. MUM, THE SUIT IS AWFUL. She gave it to me, then asked me to let her know if I get any compliments when I wear it out. Obviously I'm never going to wear it. So I've had to spend time thinking of the sort of things that someone might say to someone wearing a nice suit. Plus I had to make sure that none of those comments could be open to interpretation. I don't want Mum to hear the comment and then go, 'Hmm, do you think he liked the suit, or was he being sarcastic?' My mum is super-defensive, so if I gave her a comment she didn't like, she'd ask me who'd made it. I'd panic and give the name of a mate, and then she'd add that mate to her shit list like an angry brown santa.

If my mum thinks that my brother and I have been slighted in any way, she has been known to try to hunt down the perpetrators. When I was about fourteen, I was being chased out of school by a couple of lads; my mum got out of the car and started battering them with her handbag. There's no comeback from that. At least from then on, if someone took the piss by saying, 'Oh, you're going to get your mum on me, are you?' I could actually say yes. And I know I could still call upon her and her handbag karate if I ever need to. When Mum first got herself an Instagram account, she started asking me how she could find the details of where people lived because she saw some negative comments directed at me and wanted to unleash the fury. I imagine she was worried that, if all those trolls kept having a dig at me, I wouldn't have any self-esteem left for her to tear to pieces.

I say that about my mum, but she's incredibly supportive. She just phoned me to tell me she'd seen a poster for my show *Judge Romesh* on a bus stop and it had made her emotional. Not only was this very sweet, it also made me feel pretty guilty about what I've just written about that suit. So I'm now wearing it as I write the rest of this chapter. I've had to draw the curtains.

One other thing about my mum: she is totally honest, often to a fault, which I believe is a Tamil Sri Lankan trait. She will often phone me after I've been on a TV show and say, 'What made you wear that shirt? One of the people at work said you look fat.' To my mum, that is her making sure I learn from the mistake and either take up a crash diet or throw out the offending item – or preferably both. To me, that is a cue to finish the call, defiantly put the shirt back on and try to forget that my mum and her colleagues are talking to each other about my weight. But, in search of some more impartial and hopefully more sympathetic advice, I've started seeing a counsellor. I don't know if I'm finding it useful or not yet, because obviously I'm not doing any of the things I'm supposed to do outside the sessions. I've always done this. When I was at school, my parents got me piano lessons, but I never practised. Each lesson was me seeing a piece of music for the first time and trying to play it as if I'd been practising it all week. In my defence, I didn't have a piano, but my parents told me other kids would have practised with an orange or something. I'm also seeing a physio because I injured my shoulder recently. I don't do any of the exercises she gives me either and then I have to lie when I go to the next session.

I injured my shoulder on a snowmobile when I was filming in the Arctic for the Christmas episode of *The Misadventures of Romesh Ranganathan*. We had just been out on the ice receiving training on what to do if we saw a polar bear (in summary: shit yourself and run) and were all headed back to our camp. It was then that I discovered snowmobiles are amazing fun for about the first twenty minutes of riding them, and after that you're mainly praying that you survive.

This might have something to do with the fact that I'm the absolute opposite of a speed junkie. I'm a slow junkie. I get a buzz when I come to a safe stop.

How did this affect me on the snowmobile? The speed I felt comfortable driving at was slower than that of the rest of the group, and probably only slightly faster than walking while dragging a snowmobile, which meant I kept having to thrash it for a bit to catch up. We approached the base camp, where the snow became rock. I took a wrong turn and tipped it over. Immediately everyone in the group started panicking because, as onscreen talent, my life means more than anyone else's. Which is ridiculous, but I enjoy the priority treatment and would be furious if it stopped.

This seems a good moment to point out that I'll be joking a lot in this book. I don't want to have to keep saying, 'Just kidding,' so I'm going to trust your judgement. Every time you read something even remotely offensive, just assume I'm kidding. Except now, because when I say, 'I would be furious if it stopped,' I'm *not* joking.

When I mentioned that I started going to counselling there, I genuinely hoped I'd go into an inspirational thing about *you* going to counselling or getting help if you need it, and thereby giving me a properly emotional opening to the book, something so enlightening you almost wouldn't need to read the rest. But that didn't happen. You'll find out soon enough that I'm not the guy to go to for advice.

This book, then, is not a motivating guide to living your best life. It's a collection of my stories. It's all of the stuff I think is important in my life so far, and a few things I've thrown in for a laugh. If I miss anything out, I'll include it in the second book, which will comprise all of the stories that were too shit to go into this one, but nowhere near as shit as the ones I'll put in the third. For now, Live from Bedford Stuyvesant, The Livest One, enjoy.

I.

Mass Appeal

I was a fat child. I wasn't aware of this when I was very young as my parents would always tell me how good-looking I was. Now I wonder whether, through parental love or pure delusion, they couldn't see I wasn't. I'm not saying I was ugly, I'm just saying I was more fat than good-looking. If I was sitting in the audience of *Question Time*, Dimbleby wouldn't say, 'A question from the good-looking kid.' He'd say, 'Yes, the chubby kid who I'm not sure is looking directly at me.'

The first time I remember being upset about being overweight was when I had to buy school uniform, aged about eight. My parents took me to the uniform shop, and the sales attendant informed them I would need a pair of trousers for a child much older than me on account of my 'unusually large waist'. I remember going to a changing room and crying while trying on a pair of trousers that must have been made for Pavarotti to grow into. My being the size I was meant that my mum often had to shorten the legs by about two feet to avoid me pushing the concept of turn-ups far beyond acceptable levels.

My dietary habits became of concern to my school, but never to my parents. My mum was a feeder. She loved nothing more than to see my brother and me tucking into the hog roast she had prepared as a mid-morning snack. This isn't an attempt to blame my parents completely for my childhood obesity, as my brother managed to avoid being overweight, which leads to the conclusion that I was just a greedy bastard.

My mum actively avoided doing anything about it. She used to pack me jam sandwiches to take to school. Not for lunch: I was having school dinners. They were for break time. The other children ran off to play football, but I didn't have time for that as I had four rounds of sandwiches to smash through. My shirt was rarely free of crumbs. The school became so concerned that they contacted Mum to let her know she probably shouldn't be giving me so much food for break. She responded immediately by telling me to find somewhere to hide when I was eating my sandwiches.

This wasn't as much Mum's fault as the fault of Sri Lankan culture. Sri Lanka is one of those places where if your guests don't eat, regardless of the time of day or circumstance, you are declared unfit to be a homeowner and cast out into the street. You then visit other people in their homes, hope they don't offer you any food, and take over their place. Please be aware that not everything written here is factually correct.

I remember, as a child, popping round to drop off a gift at the house of one of Mum's friends. It was a five-minute walk. If the gift was anything like the suit she got me, definitely not worth it. When I got there I would say hello awkwardly, hand over the gift, and return home. My mum's friend had other plans: I was ushered into the dining room, where he insisted on giving me something to eat. I refused repeatedly, but I was told it would be an insult to leave without accepting his hospitality. What added to the tension was that he was making something for me that I had never eaten before – a vegetable *koicha*. I was used to being fed Sri Lankan dishes I hadn't tried before, but it was ten thirty a.m.

I waited in the man's dining room while he prepared the *koicha*. This took about half an hour. I remember sitting there, silently cursing my mum. Errands were expected to be completed without complaint at my house – Mum would often remind us that doing an errand was a pretty small ask when you consider that she'd brought us into the world. She would articulate that sentiment at length and at volume, and you could sometimes leave the room and complete the task while she was in the middle of one of her rants about you not doing anything.

The man walked into the dining room with the meal he had prepared, which smelt very familiar. And that was probably because *koicha*, rather than being a Sri Lankan speciality, was how he pronounced 'quiche'.

So I was eating a mid-morning quiche (delicious BTW) in front of my mum's friend, who had not made anything for himself. He just wanted to be sure I enjoyed it. So he sat and watched me eat. Going back to that memory does seem a bit dodgy now. A man watching a fat kid eat some quiche in silence. But that was just him being hospitable. I think.

Being a fat child meant I had very little attention from girls. This was made painfully obvious when a friend of mine suggested to a girl we knew that she and I become girlfriend and boyfriend and she laughed. Not a cute, coy laugh of young attraction. She laughed in the awkward way you might when you're trying not to look upset at being the victim of a cruel prank. I realized then that I was going to have to work extremely hard on my personality. That didn't really work out.

I've never been great with girls. I remember once being on a school trip with the first girl of my dreams – Sarah Elliot. She was divine: she had a smile that made my heart tremble, and her hair was a deep brunette that seemed to radiate gorgeousness. She was also one of only two girls in the class and the other had seen me in swimming trunks in a PE lesson, so I assumed I was down to a choice of one. I'm not saying I looked bad in swimming trunks, but they were so tight that when I emerged from the changing rooms my PE teacher looked at me and actually winced. As if it was *his* balls in the vice-like grip of a pair of under-sized Speedos.

So, Sarah was to be the victim of my affections. I managed to end any chances with her, though, on the aforementioned school trip. That's not to say things had gone brilliantly up to that point. I'm fairly sure I'd been a mild embarrassment to her for some time already. I rarely spoke to her directly, but spent much of my time trying to be in the same vague area as she was. Which meant she basically had a stalker, but one that would always keep a safe distance.

The school trip was to France, to a place called L'École Hampshire. We were nine years old, and the school had sent us there to improve our French. L'École Hampshire was beautiful, some might say romantic, and I set about trying to ingratiate myself with Sarah by continuing to hang around in the same area as her. (I myself had been the victim of someone 'hanging around in my area'. When I was at university, I went on a European student conference to Hungary. A girl from Lithuania had taken a shine to me. I am not saying this was because of the novelty 'brown factor', but she would often say things like 'I have never been with man who skin looks like yours. It lovely.' During one of the meetings I had a bit of dodgy stomach, and was passing quite a lot of gas. I decided to spare the group and move over to another area of the building and pretend I was looking at a painting. Unfortunately, my new admirer noticed, and decided to join me just as I had dropped something nuclear. Bearing in mind her limited interactions with people of colour, I can only assume she now thinks we all smell like that. She certainly didn't talk to me for the rest of the trip. I didn't want to go out with her, but I definitely didn't want her to leave me alone because I smelled like a rotting whale.)

It was during my trip to France that I had two of possibly the most embarrassing experiences of my entire life, which perhaps explains why my French to this day veers somewhere between pitiful and non-existent.

The first experience centres around some students from another school, who were also there for the week. There was obviously some friction, exacerbated by the fact that they were state-school kids and we were little posh twats. I, however, being the chameleon that my lazy eye and girth had trained me to be, was able to straddle both camps. I remember being at a barbecue and talking to one of the kids about racism. I told him the complete untruth that racist comments never bothered me. (This fails to take into account the time that someone called me a 'chocolate drop' and I cried for nearly two hours without a break even to eat my jam sandwiches.) The lad thought this was impressive, and we decided to play a practical joke on everyone: he would say racist things to me, I would pretend to be upset, and when everyone was appalled, we would reveal it was a joke, everyone would laugh and we would be responsible for uniting the two schools. To this day, I have no real idea of the motivation behind this plan. I'm guessing now that the benefit to me was making my lie about immunity to racism come true, and the benefit to him was that he had a golden ticket to be racist. Little did he know that Twitter would soon come along and give these golden tickets to everybody to use as much as they want.

The reality proved to be very different, for two reasons. The first was that he decided to get a couple of friends to take part as well, and second, I found the racism deeply upsetting. And not even after a while. Immediately. Which meant that what followed was about half an hour of four or five boys being horribly racist to me and me just crying my eyes out – for real. The problem was that the boys thought I was still following the plan, so the more upset I got, the more hilarious they thought it was. As my crying got louder, they were inspired to up the ante. They only finished when my crying produced a noise that sounded like a lilo deflating and they began to suspect I wasn't acting.

It was a pretty horrible thing for a teacher to stumble across, and even worse, I was so upset that I didn't initially reveal my cooperation. This meant that all three boys were roundly bollocked and sent to their rooms as I watched. I imagine the racist things they said paled by comparison to the racist things they were then thinking. The two schools were also far from united. It was an hour later, when I revealed my part, that I was sent to apologize to the 'L'École Hampshire Three'. By then their entire school hated me and the children from my own school were finding me pretty distasteful as well. I imagine Sarah watched the whole thing while wondering where we'd live when we got married.

This was a pretty unpleasant experience, but if you were to tell me I had a choice between what happened then and what was to happen later in the trip, I would have clung to the racist prank like *Love Island* contestants cling to celebrity. If Sarah was still clinging to any vestiges of attraction, I was soon to extinguish them completely and quite dramatically.

It was the last day of the trip and we were all about to have a long coach ride to the airport. We were allowed to stock up at the school tuck shop before leaving. I purchased many, many chocolates and a bottle of cola, and proceeded to spend the journey working on achieving type 2 diabetes. After finishing the snacks, I felt really great – confident, even. That may have been the sugar rush, but I didn't care as it meant I finally plucked up the courage to engage Sarah in some witty banter. My God, I was charming. Every sentence was a punchline. Anything anybody said was hammered over the boundary for six as I smashed jokes around the bus for the entire journey. It remains to this day one of my best ever gigs. Sarah was laughing at me and playing with her hair – at one point she even touched my arm. I was buzzing. I even made a joke about the racism prank that went down brilliantly.

It turns out that this entire experience was put in place by the gods to build me up to a sufficient height for the crushing fall that was to follow. As we pulled into the airport, I became horribly aware that the cola had worked its way through my system and was demanding immediate release. I wouldn't have minded as much if this had happened gradually, but my need-a-pissometer went from 0 to 100 almost immediately.

I wasn't massively worried as we were pulling up and toilets would be available soon but, as is the nature of school trips, everything took a lot longer than anticipated. We had to wait for all of the bags to be unloaded, then we had to wait for them to be allocated, then we had to figure out where the twat kid who always went missing had got to. This was all while my bladder had more and more rivets pinging off it, while I was still trying to be charming and hilarious.

You are probably assuming you know how this is going to end and you're right, except the way it happened was much, much worse. What's worse than pissing yourself in front of the love of your life? Let me tell you – pissing yourself as you arrive at the toilet. That's right. A few of us were in the same predicament and all headed to the airport toilet, but as my hand touched the door, my brain said, 'Thank goodness – we've made it,' and I proceeded to release every drop of piss available as I stood there in the doorway.

I continued inside as if this had not just happened. My

friends were all commenting on how lucky it was we had got there in time when I pointed out to them that in fact I hadn't. I was so upset that I actually pointed out to people that I had wet myself. If that isn't rock bottom I don't know what is. In fairness to my friends, they went to the teachers, with me distraught in the toilets, and brought me my suitcase so that I could change. They never mentioned it again, I imagine because it was too pathetic – it would have been like kicking a stray dog. My hopes that Sarah might not have noticed were dashed by the fact that (a) she had seen the whole thing play out at the toilet door, and (b) I was wearing a different-coloured pair of trousers when I walked back out to join the group. She found it almost impossible to make eye contact with me on the plane. Partly because of my lazy eye. But mainly because nobody wants to be associated with the piss-pants boy.

2.

Could the Real Romesh Ranganathan Please Stand Up?

I did my second ever gig at the Comedy Café in Shoreditch. I was thirty-one. I'd decided I was going to give comedy a go. I wasn't doing it thinking I could make any money or it could eventually become a career, I just thought it would be fun to give it a try. I was a teacher at the time, and I think I was actually aspiring to be a failed or frustrated artist of some kind, in the way all teachers are. Everyone seemed to spend their evenings failing in a band, failing at stand-up, or failing to maintain a stable home life.

My first gig was at a Pontin's holiday camp when I was nine. They had a talent competition and I decided to enter as a stand-up, with a book of jokes I took all of my material from. I don't know if this was specific to the book I owned, but a lot of the jokes at that time seemed to have no problem playing with the stereotype of Irish people being stupid. The jokes were incredibly racist, but the bigger crime here, comedy-wise, was that my set was entirely built on stolen material.

There was a joke where a man is buying a Rolls-Royce and is a bit short of cash. He goes out into the street to see if someone can lend him 10p to make up the price. He bumps into an Irish man – we know he's Irish because his name is Paddy. Paddy says, 'Here's twenty p. Buy me one as well.'

The point of that joke is that Paddy is incredibly stupid because he'd assumed that Rolls-Royces cost 10p. Stupid Paddy, I thought, when I read it. I'd never even met an Irish person but I had the clear impression that they were all thick – and the Pontin's crowd seemed to agree, the joke went down a storm. Two years later, aged eleven, I came back to that book and was able to apply the modicum of scrutiny required to deconstruct the gag. First of all, what kind of gangster is buying that car in cash? Second, if you're spending that kind of money and the staff aren't willing to give you a 10p discount, I would really question how much those guys want the sale. All things considered, upon being confronted with a guy asking for 10p to buy a Rolls-Royce, the most likely assumption is that they'd been discounted to 10p each. Paddy appears to be the only person in the whole scenario who is making any sense at all.

That was one of the many hugely racist jokes that I told as part of my set that night at Pontin's, Camber Sands, which I also delivered completely in a Sri Lankan accent – a very early recognition of the fact that my ethnic-minority roots could be exploited for comedic value.

That night I won the competition. There were only two other contestants, and one was a girl playing a kazoo. She was shit but at least she was performing her own material. I can't remember what the other guy did, which suggests it was less entertaining than the kazoo act. But I didn't care, because this fat Asian kid reading out loud in a fake accent blew them both out of the water. I'm not saying I smashed the gig. What I *am* saying is that my act clearly displayed exactly the level of racial intolerance that is ideal for a crowd at a British holiday park.

Twenty-two years later I decided to capitalize on that Pontin's buzz. I googled 'comedy night' and found the Comedy Café. They had a new-act session on a Wednesday, and you could phone up for a spot. I called them and was told by a very nice lady that you were only allowed to do the show if you had done twenty or more gigs before. I lied and was immediately booked in for that week. They obviously had that rule to keep the calibre of comedy high, and so nobody shit could turn up and make a tool of themselves. I was so naïve that I thought I could walk in and compete on a bill with established acts without anyone noticing. Turns out that was as likely as buying a Rolls-Royce for 10p.

I didn't tell anyone about the gig except my wife. It felt embarrassing to me. As if I was saying, 'I really believe I'm good enough to go onstage and be funny for strangers.'

There is no such thing as a humble stand-up comedian. You're arrogant by default for thinking you're so funny and entertaining that people should pay money to see you do it. That seems incredible to me, even now. There is a massive difference between being funny to your mates and doing stand-up comedy. 'Having a go' at stand-up is basically like saying, 'You know how I was funny the other night at the pub? I've decided my talent is so strong I can monetize it.' And I wasn't even funny generally. I would often take the piss out of my friends, and I had a reputation for never losing in a slanging match, but I wasn't the life and soul of any party. That was much more my brother, and people often openly wonder how the hell I ended up being the one with the comedy career.

It still happens. I'll be at the pub with mates, and if there is ever a new person who's come along they will at some point say, 'I thought you'd be funnier than this.'

And I usually just sadly say, 'Did you? Sorry.' And then there's an awkward silence before they decide not to talk to me again, and I am hugely relieved.

If I was arrogant in my decision to try stand-up, I was even more arrogant in my approach to the gig. I'm ashamed to say I assumed it would come easily to me. In hindsight I can see the Pontin's victory had gone to my head.

I imagine that's what everybody starting stand-up believes. The best stand-ups make it look easy, which has the unfortunate side effect of making everybody believe that it is. I'm sure it is to some people – I can't imagine that Frank Skinner ever found it difficult – but I suspect most people try it, find it incredibly difficult, then spend their entire careers hoping it will become as easy as it seemed the day before they started.

My set list contained routines on Christian Bale's voice in *Batman*, going to a gym with an open-air café that wafted the smell of food across the workout area, and trying to buy a smutty magazine from a twenty-four-hour petrol station. More on that later. I had worked out the *Batman* bit in advance and run through it with my wife, and I remember using the words 'husky paedophile' as part of it. It was pretty impressive stuff.

I still stand by that *Batman* material, although I never did it again. I have no idea why Christian Bale decided on that voice. I get that Batman would disguise his voice. In fact, I think it's a pretty amazing idea, as I don't recall many super-heroes having done it before. I can't believe that Superman doesn't do it. The man takes off his glasses, and doesn't think to change his voice even a little bit. I know that Superman was originally conceived in the 1930s, but surely even then everyone knew who people were when they took their glasses off. I can't think of a single situation where I've had my glasses on, taken them off and people have said, 'Excuse me, mate, do you know where Romesh went?' I actually think Superman would be a lot more entertaining if when Clark Kent took off his glasses he adopted an accent to help with the disguise. I would love to see Superman rock up and say 'Whagwan now Lex Luther you dirty lickle bumba claat?'

I wrote a lot of the set on the train on the way to the gig. My cocky attitude was starting to give way to nerves, and I was terrified that I wouldn't have enough material. So I wrote and wrote, without it occurring to me that I would struggle to remember it all.

I arrived, and became immediately aware that I had made a mistake. The other comics on the bill hadn't lied: they actually had gig time under their belts. They all knew each other too, and were chatting excitedly about the evening ahead. They looked so ensconced in conversation that I felt too intimidated to approach them and sat on my own in another corner of the club. I then spent a good hour trying to decide whether or not to run away. I looked over and over the jokes I'd written down. There is a magical unexplainable phenomenon that still works to this day where, however funny you think the material you've written is, as soon as you turn up to a gig to try it out, it fades and becomes almost incoherent.

I have had gigs where, having taken a notebook onstage to try out new material, the words have faded and disappeared, while a voice in my head repeatedly says, *'Everybody knows you're crap.'*

Gradually the club started to fill. The people looked terrifying – comedy connoisseurs who were going to hate everything I was doing. I was properly shitting myself, but still trying to cling to the remaining five per cent of me that was convinced I was absolutely going to smash this gig.

I can't remember any of the acts that went on before me. I just remember my name being called and going onstage, trying to look supremely confident. It had been expressed to me repeatedly by the organizers that we had five minutes each. I wasn't aware of (a) how long five minutes feels onstage, (b) how selfish it is to overrun when lots of acts are on, and (c) how not to be shit at stand-up comedy.

I started my set with my Sri Lankan accent, the only legacy of my infamous Pontin's appearance, and proceeded to deliver my material. My plan was to reveal partway through the set that I don't actually have a Sri Lankan accent. I imagined this would lead to the audience collapsing in fits of laughter, before I was carried out on their shoulders, and the owner of the Comedy Café informed me that I was the best comedian he'd ever seen.

What actually happened was that I did my big reveal and it got absolutely nothing. Then I remembered I'd accidentally nicked the idea off Omid Djalili. This was a lot of information to process during my second time onstage and I quickly descended into a panicked garble. I overran very badly. I went on for such a long time that the guy running the night flicked the stage lights on and off to signal to me that I'd outstayed my welcome. I know this now, but I didn't realize at the time why the lights had flickered, and proceeded to deliver some witty riffs about the electricity failing. This was delivered to more silence. I then said my thank-yous and left the stage to the sort of rapturous applause that you might expect if you started juggling at a funeral. People were just grateful I'd finished.

I sat and watched the rest of the acts, and most of them were just a blur as I was completely off my tits on adrenalin. I do remember one act. Catie Herring – then Catie Wilkins – delivered a set about a boyfriend asking her to talk dirty in bed. It was incredible, and really hammered home to me that I didn't have a clue what I was doing – both as a comedian and in the bedroom.

The night was a competition of sorts, and after all of the acts had been on there was a break for the judges to deliberate before the winner was announced and invited to come back on to do a longer set. During the break I went outside for a cigarette. I didn't particularly want to smoke, but I wanted to be around members of the audience, in the hope that someone would approach me and tell me what they'd thought of my jokes.

My dream came true when a young bloke came up to me and asked me how long I'd been going. 'To be honest, that was actually my first ever gig,' I said proudly. I'd decided to discount Pontin's to make me sound more impressive. He took a long drag of his cigarette, as if to suggest he required the nicotine to process his thoughts on what I'd done. I was very excited.

He exhaled. 'You had a lot of confidence, but you went on for ages and I can't remember you telling a single joke.'

'Ah, cool, thanks,' I replied, pretending that what he'd said hadn't taken a massive shit on my self-esteem.

I knew I wasn't going to win that night because Catie had smashed it, but I think I was at least hoping for some sort of honourable mention. Perhaps something along the lines of 'Well, I think we can all tell he was inexperienced, but we know we witnessed the birth of one of the all-time greats tonight.'

It didn't happen. Catie was declared the winner and then I left, without the organizers talking to me, probably because they were furious at how badly I'd gone over my time.

Overrunning is something I never do now. Audiences have a finite amount of attention, and for you to take more of it than you're supposed to is basically you deciding that you're more important than the acts that are due to go on after you. My laziness means I'm far more likely to go under my time. If I ever turn up at a gig and the promoter says, 'We're running a bit late. Do you mind doing fifteen minutes instead of twenty?' it's as much as I can do not to become aroused. If they told me the gig was cancelled completely, I would probably orgasm.

That makes it sound as if I don't enjoy doing comedy. That's not the case. It's just that the longer you're onstage the more opportunity you have to die on your arse. If you're given less time, the probability of you leaving the stage and crying on the train home is lessened. That is always my ultimate aim: avoid humiliation.

I did some proper research before my next gig. I looked into open-mic nights, how you should take things slowly and build up your act. I realized I'd probably played it pretty badly by taking on a gig I wasn't ready for. I also realized I'd blacklisted my name at the Comedy Café for quite some time. On the plus side, I'd got some stage time under my belt and a possible introduction to Omid Djalili if he wanted to have a go at me for ripping off his material.

My next gig was in Brighton – an open-mic night called 'Top Banana' that took place in a basement under a café. I messaged the promoter, Bola Ajani, and she put me on for the next available date.

This time round I told my brother, who in turn told some friends, and before I knew it we had a group of ten people all heading to Brighton. I was grateful for their support, but I really didn't want people to come and watch me: even though I didn't know how shit I was, I did know I was quite shit.

Determined to improve from my low base, I did a lot more preparation this time around. I worked up some of the material I'd done at the Comedy Café, then trimmed it to a five-minute set and practised it repeatedly at home, using a comb as a microphone. This was essentially my *Rocky* montage moment; except with Rocky practising for his gig and forgetting to mark his Year 9 class homework.

There are advantages to practising the set at home: you memorize what you want to say, you figure out how to hit the lines, you time exactly how long it will be, allowing space for laughs, and you go to the gig feeling a little bit more in control. The disadvantage is that you're repeatedly saying the material to silence and losing confidence in it every time you do it. I remember asking my wife to sit and watch me do the set in the living room. The exhilaration I felt when she sat through it completely straight-faced, then said, 'Yeah, that was fine,' will never leave me.

We rocked up at the gig, I introduced myself to Bola, then settled at the back with my entourage to watch the other acts. My set had the Batman stuff, how you can get porn to satisfy any particular fetish you want, the gym stuff, and some topical gags about fair-trade food. I was running it through in my head as I watched the first half of the night.

I remember the compère, Mark Simmons, vividly, partly because we're still friends now, but I would have remembered him regardless. He went up onstage and owned it. He was immediately hilarious, talking to audience members, taking their responses and turning them into jokes. I had never seen that happen before and I thought my head was going to fall off.

I watched act after act, and they were either very good, or so bad that I could feel genuine anger radiating from the crowd. It was enjoyable and agonizing because I knew I had to go up soon. Sure enough, Mark called my name and, to the cheers of my entourage, I went up and delivered my set. It was a mixed bag. Some of the stuff went over okay, and at one point I actually got a laugh, which hadn't happened at the previous gig.

I came offstage feeling like a superhero. My wife, brother

and friends hugged me and told me how brilliant I was. The rest of the night went by in a blur, and I went home feeling ecstatic.

When we got in, my wife told me that, although I'd been quite funny, I'd touched my glasses too much, moved around in a distracting way and garbled some of my punchlines. That was the beginning of my wife providing me with some of the most useful feedback I've received throughout my career. She's incredibly supportive and always honest – she tells me exactly what she thinks. During the early days, she helped me improve a lot. But while her notes on delivery were tip-top, her opinions on my material demonstrated a breathtaking lack of understanding of humour. Let's see how she likes that feedback.

The next day, I was pleasantly surprised to receive a message from Bola saying she'd enjoyed my set. She gave me a list of names, contacts who might book me for more gigs around the Brighton area. I messaged them all, and pretty soon I had a schedule of gigs locked in for the next few weeks. I started to feel like I was getting somewhere. I even allowed myself to hope that I could get good enough to have my Comedy Café ban lifted.

I proceeded to gig all over Brighton, to varying degrees of success. The problem with starting out in stand-up is that the adrenalin of performing often blinds you to the quality of what you're doing. I was shit, but I was enjoying it.

The other thing I didn't grasp was that I was supposed to work on my material and polish it at the different gigs. I'd begun to notice that a lot of the same acts were at all of those gigs, seeing me do the same stuff every time, so I decided I had to write a brand new set for every performance. That made the gigs incredibly stressful. Every time I did one, I'd spend the day writing, tweaking and memorizing, then trying not to have a panic attack at the venue as all of the words left my head.

One week, I had two gigs and wrote two separate sets. Another act was also booked for both gigs. *What if he smashes them and I die twice?*, I thought.

I turned up for the first, at Top Banana again, with a set I'd prepared on people who grow their own fruit and vegetables. I have no idea why I was talking about that: I don't recall ever having a genuine opinion on the subject. I went up and delivered whatever I could remember from what I'd written. It went okay. There was a particularly terrible bit when I talked about not wanting to eat fruit that had been fertilized with human excrement, and that I would only eat a strawberry that had been grown in this way if it looked like Cheryl Cole.

Then I watched the guy doing the same gigs go up and smash it. One—nil to him.

A few days later, I went to the next show with my brother and parents. The gig was at the Prince Arthur pub in Brighton, run by a man who continues to be a friend, Aidan Goatley. He greeted all of the acts with frightening enthusiasm. It was the night before Valentine's Day so I'd put together a set on the differences between men and women when it came to love. This was cutting-edge stuff. There was no ground I wasn't prepared to break.

During the set I took the pretty low move of ripping into my dad. I try not to have a go at audience members unless they deserve it, but back then I had no such scruples. It wasn't that I was less principled, just desperate for any sort of laughs. Dad had to listen to his son listing all of the ways in which he looked like a budget James Brown. My poor, supporting, loving father just sat there taking a pasting from me, having offered no provocation whatsoever. I then delivered my planned set, during which I completely forgot what I was meant to say and stood silently on the stage for what felt like days. The audience were forgiving and I regained my composure, but I imagine Dad was delighted to have his revenge so quickly. He didn't say anything as I sat down next to him to watch the other acts.

Again the standard was high and people did very well. And then the man who had become, this week at least, my arch nemesis stepped up. He smashed it yet again, with exactly the same set he'd delivered a few days previously. Two—nil to him – and he'd taught me a useful lesson. I wasn't getting better because I was refusing to review and polish what I'd done at the gig before. I was just blasting out new set after new set, forgetting words, shouting at my dad, when I should have been looking at how I'd done and trying to better it the next time.

After the gig Aidan approached me. 'You did a completely different set from last time. What was the thinking behind that?' Which is a very polite way of saying 'You really don't have a fucking clue what you're doing, do you?'

There were some pretty low points during those early gigs, which often disguised themselves as high points. I did a Brighton gig with a set about the masks they were handing out when bird-flu was supposed to be on its way. I'd been watching the news with the sound down: the footage, I said, looked like an intensive Mexican ninja recruitment policy. I still stand by that. Maybe we'll have another bird-flu scare and I can revive the routine.

A lovely man by the name of Alex Dawson saw me at the gig and offered me a spot at a night he ran in Southampton. This felt like a breakthrough because it was the first time I'd got a gig without having to ask. I accepted, and the following week I was in a car with a teacher friend, Mark Lotsu, heading to the club.

I owe Mark a lot. He was so enthusiastic about me doing comedy that he must have come to every gig I did in the first year. After I left teaching to go full-time as a stand-up, we drifted apart a bit as I got so busy. This is something I would later come to regret. He must have had the lowest possible opinion of my comedy. He saw me die in all sorts of locations and in all sorts of ways. He was so hugely supportive, and would religiously post about my gigs and say things like 'He is going to be the next big thing.' Outside my family, he was probably the first person to show genuine faith in what I was doing.

On that occasion, we were both in a great mood. It was the furthest we'd driven for a gig and we were both looking forward to seeing what the whole thing was like. We pulled up early and found the bar. As we walked in a girl at the door was collecting money for the comedy night. 'Are you Romesh? Alex told me loads about your set – look forward to seeing you.'

Holy shit, bruv. Not only had I got myself an out-of-town

gig, but the girl had heard about my act. This was next level! I walked into the venue, trying not to pimp-strut to the back of the room. Instead, I should have looked for some sort of disguise because I died on my arse that night. I died so hard that I wasn't sure they'd applaud me off. I died so hard that people started worrying about stand-up comedy as an art form. I died so hard you could have heard a pin drop, and the sound of it hitting the floor would've been funnier than anything I'd said onstage. I died so hard that the girl at the door couldn't bring herself to make eye contact, let alone speak to me, for the rest of the evening.

The journey back from that gig was horrendous. Mark and I sat in near silence, save for a few comments from me on how humiliating it had been. Mark assured me it hadn't been that bad and tried to change the subject. He had driven me for over two hours to the show, then had to counsel me all the way back. I got home and sat on the end of my bed with my head in my hands. I was devastated. My wife woke up, looked at me, and said, 'If it makes you feel like this, maybe you should stop.' And I knew she was right, but also that I never would.*

* This isn't true. I just thought it would be a cool way to end the chapter.

3.

Started from the Bottom
Now We're Here

I was watching the film *Hop* at home with the children in 2012. The main character in the story, a rabbit voiced by Russell Brand, had fallen on hard times and declared, 'Maybe this is the rags part of my rags-to-riches tale.' I don't know if it was the emotion of the scene, or if I hadn't had enough sleep, but I burst into tears. I imagine I'm not the only person to have started crying during a viewing of *Hop* but that has more to do with the realization that you've just spent two hours watching a terrible film and life is finite.

The scene struck a nerve, because I really felt we were at rock bottom too. Of course, these things are all relative. Years later, I was working in Los Angeles and was telling a runner on the show about the difficulties of starting out as a comedian. He then told me about the time he'd lived in a car for a month, and washed at friends' houses. I wished he'd gone first: I would still have told him my story but I'd at least have made up a death or some sort of STI.

I had recently given up my job as a teacher, and wasn't making anywhere near enough money as a stand-up to justify that decision. I was somehow under the belief that I would be able to do more comedy without a full-time job holding me back, but things weren't adding up and I learned that you can't buy food with loads of spare time and rapidly eroding self-esteem.

My first job in education had been at Hazelwick School, which was also where I had gone as a pupil. I loved working there, but was also slightly worried that my job made me a bit of a sad bastard. I would meet people I used to go to school with and they would say, 'Yeah, I'm just back from New York – investment banking, natch – to visit the folks. You?'

And I would say, 'I work at the school we used to go to and live in the house I grew up in. Please can we end this conversation?'

I decided it was time for a change and applied for a job in a tougher school, called The Beacon, which had just come out of special measures. I had a dream of rocking up and changing the system, getting the kids onside, like a fat brown Michelle Pfeiffer in *Dangerous Minds*.

I had applied for another job before the one at The Beacon and had been asked to go along for an interview. Teaching interviews are not like regular job interviews. You turn up, have a chat and a tour of the school, then teach a lesson while someone observes you. Then they call you in for your formal interview, after which you're asked to wait while the interviewers deliberate. Eventually they call you back in and tell you there and then whether you've got the job or not. This is super-awkward when there are multiple applicants: you're waiting with these people, who you're hoping are rubbish, then each of you goes in and has to come out without giving any indication of what you've just been told. I suppose you could say something, but if you don't get the gig you're trying not to look too upset, and if you do, it feels a bit insensitive to go back out and scream, 'In your face!' at the other candidates.

On that particular day, my lesson was pretty much a disaster. The kids I had to teach were completely unresponsive. I was asking questions, nobody was offering answers. I began to suspect they'd been sedated. The small mercy was that no one was running riot. I was then taken to meet the man who would be my boss if I were to get the job. By then I wasn't feeling too confident and was keen to make a good impression: this guy would be reporting back to the powers that be. I sat down with him and he began to explain his role to me. He told me about all of his responsibilities, his style of doing things, and his work philosophy: 'Most people do this but I do things my own way,' and 'You'll see that I have a way with all of the kids here.' My desire to impress him diminished as I began to suspect that he might be a twat. I had essentially ended up in an interview with teaching's version of David Brent.

I don't normally mind twats at work. In fact, it's safe to say that, in my time, I've been one. My first job out of university was working in pensions review. I had joined with three other guys: Chris, Kev and Bob – standard guys with standard names. Except Bob. Bob's name was actually Bharat, but he called himself 'Bob' at work. Trying to assimilate by choosing an English name is common among Asians in this country. I don't quite understand the logic behind it. It's almost like you're acquiescing to potential racism. A white guy wouldn't move to India and say, 'Hello, my name is Dave, but over here I go by Rajakrishnan.'

My parents gave me 'Jonathan' to use if I felt I needed it, but the situation hasn't come up. The very idea of it makes me want to change my name to 'Romesh Paki Whiteykiller' and see how things go.

The one thing I would say for Bob is that he had chosen a name that at least shared one letter with his actual name. I once had a neighbour who introduced himself as Steve. It was a fair bit down the line that I enquired about his real name and he told me it was Gurbar, which obviously shortens to Steve.

Actually, another guy started with us, whose name escapes me. He left after a couple of weeks, but I felt he had made a fundamental error on Day One. We had been given a morning's initiation, then were taken out for lunch to a distinctly shite Chinese restaurant in Croydon. We were asked to order and told it was on the company, at which point that mad bastard ordered two main courses, one of which was lobster! I couldn't bloody believe it. I thought he'd shafted himself, but when he left I realized he probably didn't like the job and was trying to get as much as he could while he was there. I imagine him still sitting in a warehouse full of all the William Mercer stationery he probably nicked.

During our first week a woman called Elaine trained us. She was very nice and had been helping us get accustomed to the mind-numbing nature of the work. I really liked Elaine but I was able very effectively to make her hate me.

Kev and I were walking down the stairs to see her about something, when I spotted her reflection coming out of her section of the office. I thought it would be hilarious to play the 'pretend you've been caught slagging someone off' game.

So as I saw Elaine's reflection approach I said, 'Isn't Elaine fucking annoying? . . . Oh, there you are Elaine, hahahaha!'

Except Elaine didn't know I'd seen her. She thought I was slagging her off for real. She gave me a look of thunder and said, 'That was bad timing, wasn't it?' I'd had an absolute shocker. And she was not going to forget it. From then on, Elaine treated me like someone who had openly described her as being fucking annoying. I even sent Kev down to tell her it was a joke but she wouldn't have it.

On my last day I went up to her and said, 'At this stage I have no reason to lie. You know that was a joke that went wrong, right?'

And she said she didn't even remember it happening. Which means there's a good possibility she just genuinely disliked me.

Genuine dislike was what I was forming for the man sitting across from me. I didn't think he was a bad person, just that he was a tit. A tit who would potentially be my direct manager. At the end of our chat, he told me he would take me to the interview. To get there, we had to walk across the school during lesson changeover, which gave this guy the opportunity to demonstrate his full range of banter skills with the students. He was all 'Hey, hey, cheeky Samuels! What's going on with the tie? You legend!' and 'Stop! What are you doing?! Just kidding! Have an amazing day, guys!' It went on and on like this all the way to the headmaster's office. That walk convinced me there was absolutely no way I could work with the man. I was also pretty keen to find a way to guarantee I would never have to speak to him again.

I hadn't been completely sure about the school and now I'd been well and truly put off by my potential boss. The problem I then faced was that if I got the job they would tell me there and then. Which meant I'd have to reject it there and then. If I got the job, I would have to tell them I didn't want it. I could sabotage the interview, but word would spread and I'd probably have damaged my future prospects. I decided to do what I normally do, which has almost always let me down: just see what happens.

The interview itself was such a car crash that I suspected I might have solved the problem. There was a question about educational strands that I blagged my way through because I wasn't entirely sure what they were, and I managed to project a general air of incompetence, which weirdly I was distraught about. I didn't want the job, but I wanted that to be my choice rather than theirs. Then came the end of the interrogation: 'Well, Romesh, we're going to interview the other candidates now, but final question, and we have to ask this, would you accept the job if offered it?' The head teacher smiled as he waited for my confirmation, and looked visibly shocked when I explained I wasn't sure that I would. This had required all of my courage. The head stopped smiling and said, 'May I ask why?'

What the hell was I supposed to say? I couldn't say, 'Well, it's basically because the man I chatted to earlier was a bit of a knobhead.' I made up some blather about the nature of the role, and me not being right for the school. It was all bollocks and they knew it. I now looked like I'd applied for the job as interview practice and had wasted their time.

I eventually got a job as head of sixth form and assistant head teacher at The Beacon. It was a challenging role, with kids bussed in from local estates. This was obviously a while ago now, but at the time the sixth form, which I was now in sole charge of, had been singled out by OFSTED as one of the more problematic areas of the school. I had also been told that behaviour there was an issue. It seemed the perfect place for my Michelle Pfeiffer moment. It's fair to say, however, that the school had apparently shielded me from some of the most challenging elements of the job.

When I'd gone for my interview, I'd met the head teacher and, in a separate chat, a group of sixth-formers. I thought that was a really nice thing to do, and it made me see the school was child-centred, which is exciting for any teacher. I was also taken on a tour, and found the behaviour in every classroom to be fine, so much so that I almost couldn't believe that The Beacon had attracted such a damning OFSTED report.

When I went on to work there, I learned that when visitors came round a member of senior staff would often go just ahead of the tour, barking at children in all of the classrooms to make sure they were impeccably behaved for that period. They would sometimes even place tiny stickers on the walls in the corridors so that the person taking the tour would know exactly which route to follow and which classrooms to step into. This sort of thing probably happens at schools around the country all the time, but it seemed unbelievable. Except it was believable and I totally fell for it.

My first day was a culture shock. I was given a bottom set

year-nine class to teach and had been warned that they would be my most challenging students. I was shitting myself. I was trying to establish my authority at a new school and was about to teach a class that was considered bad even by the standards of a school that had just come out of special measures.

I walked into the classroom to find the kids throwing stuff, jumping on desks and swearing, completely ignoring me. I put my laptop on the desk and asked them to sit down. They didn't. I asked louder. Ignored again. I shouted, and a kid told me to chill out. They carried on. Not a great start.

I went to each child one by one, told them to sit down, gave them an exercise book and asked them to write their name. It took me twenty minutes to get them ready to start the lesson. Then I tried to begin, but as I went to speak a kid shouted, 'No!' I asked him what the problem was and he said he didn't have one. I went to speak again, and again he shouted, 'No!' I could see the rest of the class getting excited, like a pride of lions discovering a buffalo with a dodgy leg. To give credit to this kid, he had demonstrated an incredibly effective disruption technique. A nonsensical repeated interruption is the most difficult thing to deal with, and if nothing else, he would have a great future as a comedy-club heckler.

What happened next showed me just how precarious the authority of a teacher is. I said to him, 'I'm sorry, but if you keep interrupting me like that, you will no longer be allowed to take part in the lesson.' A classic move from Ranganathan: remove the attention-seeker from the arena.

'I don't want to be in your fucking lesson,' he said.

Well played, mate. I'd never encountered that before. At

Hazelwick, even though I had faced challenging behaviour, the children had always hated being sent out. Which meant that you always had that weapon in your arsenal. What I had never dealt with before was that many of the children at this school didn't want to be there at all, and rather than constantly exclude them, the challenge was to try to engage them and inject some enthusiasm into them for education. Much like Michelle Pfeiffer did in *Dangerous Minds* by wearing a leather jacket and being patronizing about the ghetto.

At the end of the school day, I walked to the back gate, which was one of my new 'duties'. At Hazelwick I'd volunteer for lunch duty: in exchange for losing a lunchtime watching children occasionally get boisterous in the playground, you'd get to eat school lunches, which were banging. I started to put on a lot of weight as a result of smashing through the tray-bake puddings with custard.

Years later those puddings came back to haunt me, and got me into an altercation with none other than Prue Leith, she of *Great British Menu* and *Bake Off* fame. I was doing a Radio 4 show called *The Museum of Curiosity* with *QI* impresario and general intellectual John Lloyd, and I was the curator for that series. Phil Jupitus, Prue Leith and criminologist Roger Graef were the guests. I don't know if this comes across from that list, but I had the distinct suspicion that I was out of my depth. I spent the whole series worrying about my relative lack of intelligence. It's not so much that I feel stupid, which I often do: it's more to do with the fact that I'm not as well read as I'd like to be, and have to Joey-Tribbiani-nod my way through certain conversations.

This particular episode saw me taking my usual role of cultural philistine, as Prue and Phil exchanged stories about culinary delights. I asked Prue what she thought about tray-bakes. She said they were nice and moved on.

Later in the show, she was talking about cooking guinea fowl for the royals and how difficult it was to get the meal ready. 'You wouldn't have had that problem with tray-bakes,' I said. She looked at me, visibly annoyed, and said, 'This isn't a good running joke.' Phil pissed himself laughing, and an awkward atmosphere filled the studio, the audience shifting in their seats.

A little later on, John asked Prue what her best meal had been. She told a beautiful story about eating something abroad as the sun moved beneath the horizon. I waited patiently for her to finish, and as she got to the end of her emotional tale, I said, 'That's how I felt the first time I tried a tray-bake.' Don't expect to see me on *Bake Off* anytime soon. And if you do, I'll be making tray-bakes.

When I moved to The Beacon, as assistant head teacher I was on gate duty, which meant two of the caretaking staff and I were supposed to stand there and make sure the kids weren't acting up as they were leaving. I was wandering over to the two caretakers when I saw a kid riding his bike across the playground, which wasn't allowed. I went over to him and told him to get off. He told me to piss off and rode away. The two caretakers were laughing. I discovered from them that the purpose of gate duty wasn't to stop kids acting up. It was to stand there and pretend that was what you were doing because the kids couldn't care less what you said to them. Not even if you were the assistant head teacher. So, every afternoon I would stand with the two guys while kids would walk past doing whatever they liked. We were like police officers at Notting Hill Carnival who are supposed to be looking out for weed. I imagine we would have got involved if there was some sort of stabbing, but not if it was beyond the school gates. Our non-intervention strategy was taken to its limit when it snowed. The caretakers and I spent our duty dodging snowballs that were being pelted at us from over the fence. Naturally, we did nothing to try and stop the abuse.

I make all of this sound like a nightmare, but the school had the best intentions and the truth is I found it incredibly rewarding. Those children were challenging, and every day was tough, but not as tough as their backgrounds. Many of them had awful home lives and it was amazing that they were turning up at school at all. Even though it felt glacial in pace, I made progress with those who did. I even managed to get that year-nine class engaged and working, and felt absolutely incredible to have done so. It still took me ten to fifteen minutes to get them settled at the top of the lesson, but I really felt like I'd got them onside. That lad from the first lesson even stopped shouting 'No!' every time I spoke. Although the challenges were harder than at Hazelwick, the rewards were so much bigger as well. I actually felt like I was making a difference. Maybe I *was* Michelle Pfeiffer.

The biggest demand of the job was undoubtedly the lack of engagement, and in sixth form in particular, the low aspirations of the students because of the lives they were leading. When I was at Hazelwick, we had put on an annual evening where we explained the university application process, telling the parents how they could fund higher education, and the deadlines involved. It was always a very pleasant experience, and we would end the night with some wine, nibbles and parents thanking us for being so informative. I decided to set that evening up at The Beacon. The head warned me that it wouldn't go as smoothly as it had done at my previous school. I've made that sound a little Mafia-esque, but she was telling me in an encouraging way – she didn't want me to be disappointed.

Her prophecy proved to be only too accurate. I explained the process of applying for universities and then opened it up for questions. Where previously I had been asked 'What are the Oxbridge deadlines?' and 'How come you're so great at this?', this time round I was fielding questions like 'Why the hell is this so expensive?', 'What is the point of my son doing this when he can just come and work for me?' 'Why are you telling us this when we don't want our kids going to university?' and 'Why the fuck have you pro-vided cheese?' It very much hammered home how difficult this job was going to be.

My time at The Beacon coincided with my comedy starting to pick up. I don't mean pick up in terms of mak-ing any money: I just started to gig a lot. In comedy you're running at a loss for the early years of your career, but even to come close to making ends meet, you're extremely busy. I would often finish school, jump into my car and drive up north for a ten-minute spot at a club for them to see if I was any good. I would, often as not, die on my arse, then get home to mark books.*

On one occasion I did a ten-minute spot at the Glee in Birmingham, one of a group of Glee venues, which are considered 'Premier League' in terms of clubs to get in with. All of their stages have 'GLEE' at the back Hollywood-style, the clubs are usually rammed with very nice crowds and the staff are great. And so are the line-ups. And the money's good. So everyone is desperate to get in. They always let a newer act have ten minutes at the weekend as a way of bringing them into the main line-ups, and I'd been given a spot at the Birmingham club on that particular night. I drove straight there from school, bricking it with nerves.

The compère was Michael Legge, whom I now know very well but I was meeting him for the first time. He was very kind to me, but when you're new and going into those big clubs, everything feels so scary. Sean Percival was on first, and he was also lovely but I found him intimidating too, perhaps because he had the experience I so desperately lacked. The interval came and went, and then it was time for me to go on. Michael gave me a very nice intro and, nerves aside, everything went well. The jokes worked, and there were no lines that went to nothing. I was having a great time, and I began to think I'd be asked back.

I finished my set to decent enough applause and looked to see where Michael was. He wasn't coming out. I didn't understand it. I realized I couldn't stay there for ever so I

* The last bit is a lie. I marked very rarely, and used to get bollocked for that quite a lot.

walked offstage, to find to my dismay that the door had disappeared. It was only then that I heard Michael behind me and realized I'd walked the wrong way.

My next decision was insanity. Rather than retrace my steps back up and across the stage, I decided there must be some way to get to the other side without being seen. I moved behind a curtain, walked forward and got stuck, at which point I found myself looking out at the audience through the second *e* in Glee, while Michael commentated on the whole thing. I don't know what else he could have done. It would have been very difficult for him to continue the night with me trapped at the back of the stage. Finally admitting defeat, I headed back the way I'd come, hustled awkwardly across the stage, then spent the evening pretending to laugh with every single person who asked me if I knew which way the exit was.

Eventually I realized I couldn't carry on for much longer working as a senior member of staff at the school and doing comedy. Being an assistant head teacher at a school like that is more than a job. It's a lifestyle. To make real change requires you to spend every waking moment working on improving it, and I just wasn't in a position to do that. I was being mediocre at both stand-up and teaching, and that's before we get into the difficulties I was having as a father and husband. I decided I was going to have to leave the job. But I couldn't afford to abandon teaching altogether and I didn't fancy going into another new school and learning the ropes. Especially as I was starting to think I might possibly be able to make a career of comedy if I could give it enough focus.

I emailed the headmaster at Hazelwick, Gordon Parry, and asked if there was any chance of coming back in a reduced-responsibility role. He said nothing was available, but he would keep me informed.

True to his word, a few months later he got in touch to say that a junior head of sixth form role and a maths teacher vacancy might be coming available. I would have to apply as he couldn't just give me a job, but he said they'd love to see me for it. The only snag was that, because you have to give half a term's notice to leave a school, I would have to resign from The Beacon before I knew if I had the Hazelwick job. It was the day before half-term: I had to resign straight away.

I was extremely worried about the reaction to my surprise resignation but I fired off an email, explaining that the strains of the job were too much and that I wanted to take a reduced-responsibility role elsewhere. Obviously if I was being honest I would have said that I was struggling to balance the demands of the job with a comedy career, but it felt a bit embarrassing to say that. The idea of actually becoming a comedian seemed so far-fetched that I couldn't openly admit that was now my aspiration. Then I buggered off for half-term. It did feel like a dick move, because I hadn't expressed any unhappiness in the job up to this point, but I really felt I was doing the right thing: the job I was doing was important for the school, and would be much better accomplished by somebody who could devote themselves to it entirely.

The staff at The Beacon knew I did comedy, but that was purely by accident. I was trying to build recognition as a new act, and one of the most effective ways of doing that is by entering competitions. Clubs are more likely to book you if you have a couple of accolades under your belt. I had entered a comedy competition a few months earlier in a café in Brixton. If you made it through the four competitive heats, you could win two thousand pounds. The organizers were well intentioned and supportive, but didn't have any idea what they were doing. When I turned up, the café was glass-fronted, with no stage area. There was an audience of three. We competitors took turns to die on our arses, except one man who was not taking part in the contest.

Ray Presto, who has now sadly passed away, was an open-mic-circuit legend. An older gentleman, he would always turn up to gigs looking dapper, then deliver some of the worst old-school jokes I'd ever heard. He seemed always to smash it. Everybody loved him. To this day, I have no idea if what he did at the competition was deliberate or not. If it was, it was one of the finest pieces of comedy I've ever seen.

One of the comedians was doing his competition set, when behind him we all saw Ray Presto walking past the front of the café. He stopped, looked in through the window, then started doing his hair and checking out his reflection. This caused the room to fall into fits of laughter, but the comedian performing had absolutely no idea that Ray was there, and simply assumed he was suddenly roofing the gig. It was incredible. I suspected this might be a cruel joke, sabotaging another entrant in order to give himself a better chance, which would have been funny, if harsh, but then Ray put his comb back in his pocket and walked off, to complete an incredible cameo.

Unfortunately for me, the competition organizers didn't get the idea of intellectual property and put the competition sets up on YouTube without asking anybody's permission. They'd done it straight away, but it was only to bite me on the arse when I started my time at The Beacon several months later. I was handing out textbooks to my year-ten class when a kid quoted one of my jokes verbatim. And it wasn't a suitable joke. I present it for your delectation here. Please remember I had only recently started stand-up when this was delivered:

One of the stereotypes about Sri Lankans is that they all work at twenty-four-hour service stations. I remember when I was a student, I used to get horny and head to the local twenty-four-hour petrol station to pick up a copy of Asian Babes *– or as I called it,* Babes. *One day I rocked up to the counter and who should be there but my uncle Raj: 'Hello, Romesh!' So I couldn't buy a porno mag. I had to ask for a cheese and onion pasty. And do something with that.*

If you're not clear on what I'm saying in that bit I'm essentially explaining that I would be using the pasty as some sort of makeshift wanking sleeve. It's pretty terrible stuff when heard from an amateur comedian, never mind a student quoting it back to you in a lesson at your new school at which you're trying to make a good impression.

As soon as the lesson finished I ran back to my office. It was next to the sixth-form common room and was all glass, so I had the tricky issue of trying to find the video without anyone seeing what I was doing and thereby making the problem worse. As it turns out, I needn't have worried: everyone on the school site had already watched the clip. Fortunately, the head saw the funny side, but I never again ate a cheese and onion pasty in open view.

What she didn't see the funny side of, understandably, was my sudden resignation towards the end of my first year. The first day after half-term I arrived at school to find a message asking me to go and see her immediately. I knew this was going to be an unpleasant meeting, so I steeled myself for some industrial-strength awkwardness.

I walked into the office to find her sitting facing away from me, looking at her computer screen in silence. This had the effect of making me feel as though I had interrupted her even though she had asked me to come in. I guess she was playing some weird psychological game, but she was behaving like Anchorman. She told me to sit, without looking at me, which I did. The silence that followed felt eternal. I started to wonder if she had forgotten I was there, and I was just going to have to spend the day watching her at her computer. Eventually, just after my wife had called the police to report me missing, she spoke.

'When you originally sent your surprise email, you told me it was because you wanted a position of less authority. However, I have just received a reference request from Hazelwick School explaining that you're taking on a position as a junior head of sixth form there. That's responsibility, isn't it?'

Hazelwick had asked for a reference? I'd worked there for seven years! And I'd been at The Beacon for less than one. What did they need to know? Did they think I might suddenly have become a sex offender? I was processing this information when it occurred to me that I hadn't spoken for a bit and needed to respond. The truth was that the position at Hazelwick carried loads less responsibility than what I was doing at The Beacon, but I knew that was a pointless protest. My job at this stage was to accept her condemnation and bring the meeting to as quick an end as possible.

'I thought you had a bright future in education,' she continued. 'Not any more.'

It was starting to get a bit *Godfather* now and, to be honest, I felt she'd gone a bit far. But I did understand where she was coming from. She was passionate about the school, had appointed me to sort out one of their most challenging areas, and I had decided to bail without warning. I was embarrassed but, at the same time, couldn't bring myself to admit it was because of comedy. It felt incredibly selfish. What was I supposed to say? 'Well, the truth is I would have loved to continue helping out the children here, who I have come to realize need our support more than any other students I have ever encountered, but I'm quite keen to make a career out of telling jokes about shagging pasties.' I just apologized profusely and left.

For the remainder of my time at the school, my life became hell. People stopped talking to me, made me feel unwelcome at meetings, then had a go at me for not attending them. I was given the worst duties. The final kick in the balls was on my penultimate day when the school bursar called me into his office for a chat. He explained to me that the school would prefer it if I didn't turn up tomorrow and instead left quietly at the end of the day. Which meant that none of the students would be able to say goodbye. This felt horrible at the time. But I accepted it and actually admired their resolve. The head was furious with me because she cared about the school so much and they all clearly put the children first, and I could only respect that.

What I didn't know is that my life decisions would go on to upset Hazelwick as well. I think this was probably inevitable. The problem you face trying to be a comedian is that you also have to make ends meet, and my ends were further apart than those of most comedians starting out because I had a family to look after. That meant that I was trying to hold on to my day job as long as I could, but what it also meant was that I was doing that job somewhat ineffectively. I'm not proud of this. But it happened.

Returning to Hazelwick School ended up not being as much fun as I'd anticipated. The staff had changed, the government had moved the education goalposts once more, and I was working for someone who was unsure of my motivations for returning to the school at a lower position than the one I had left. Again, it felt too embarrassing to say I was happy to do so because I wanted to be a comedian. They might have seen the pasty routine.

I worked at Hazelwick for the following year and stayed on top of the job as well as doing gigs. However, more gigs led to even more, and pretty soon I was in a similar position to the one I had been in at The Beacon, struggling to juggle two careers and doing both badly. It got to a point where my boss called me into their office and told me I needed to choose between being a teacher or a comedian. I wanted to be annoyed, but they had a fair point. It's just frustrating when you're confronted with your own failings. And still I didn't admit that I had already made up my mind.

Later that year, I was given a place on the 'Big Value' Edinburgh show run by Just the Tonic. Seann Walsh had recommended me and it was a huge honour. It was a compilation show where they put on a mixed bill every night of the Fringe. You had to audition to get in and loads of comics I respected had done it. The only problem was that the Fringe runs from August right through to the beginning of September. Part of my duties as one of the sixth-form team was to attend the GCSE and A-level results days in August, so there was a clash. What should I do about it? Should I explain to the guys at Just the Tonic that I'd need the time off to go back to school? Or speak to the school's management to see if they'd allow me to miss the results days? I decided to just go ahead with Big Value, and see what happened. It was a bit of a naïve strategy. In fact, it was less a strategy and more a case of hoping that a solution would present itself. I told myself I'd figure out how to cross the enormous bridge when I came to it.

I instantly regretted my decision to put comedy first on the opening night of Big Value. I had worked rigorously on my twenty-minute set in the run-up to Edinburgh. I was on the show with Eric Lampaert, Caroline Mabey and John Robins. I was very nervous but felt pretty confident that I was sufficiently prepared to smash the shit out of the gig. That was until I died that first night. And then every night for two weeks. It was deeply embarrassing. But I did little to change the outcome. Every night I would go up and deliver exactly the same material, hoping that for some reason every previous night had been exceptionally unlucky.

This paled into insignificance, given the omnishambles I was about to create. As the month went on, the time rapidly approached when I'd have to explain to the school that I wasn't going to be there. Again, I contemplated asking for time off from Big Value. In retrospect I am sure the organizer, Darrell Martin, would have let me go – he's a very understanding and supportive guy – but I didn't want to do anything to jeopardize my comedy career.

I was also faced with the problem that I had been absolutely tanking at these gigs so my position was weakened. Had I been ripping it, I think I would have felt more comfortable about approaching Darrell for a favour, but it felt a bit like my comedy world was falling apart. I had decided to go full tilt at this thing, and now there was the distinct possibility that I wasn't very good at it.

So I decided to lie to the school. I should explain that I was desperate, and what I did does not cast me in a good light. But you're reading this to get the inside story, aren't you? Deal with it.

I didn't want to leave it to the actual exam results day and call in sick, which would have been the easiest option, because that would have left them actually short-handed, and I wanted to give them enough time to find a workable way round the situation. So I had to come up with another excuse. I told them that Leesa, my wife, had been feeling ill, possibly because of her pregnancy, and I had to stay home to look after our son and give her the help she needed. I felt absolutely awful lying like that, but I was desperate to finish Edinburgh, and try to salvage something from the opportunity I had been given, and provide the school enough notice. After I made the call, I wasn't so much relieved as overcome by a tsunami of guilt.

My experience on Big Value remains one of my regrets as a comedian. I should have taken a few risks. After the first night with a lukewarm response, I should have been looking at my set, picking out the weak points and punching it up, trying to figure out where I was going wrong. But I was scared. I worried that if I took a risk, it could backfire: I might leave myself exposed and even removed from the show, which in hindsight would have been quite handy. As it was, I continued to deliver exactly the same set in the vain hope that it would somehow get better. It didn't.

It was on my return home to Crawley that the true horror of my Edinburgh experience fully showed itself. I walked into my office in September on the first day back to find that nobody in the sixth-form team was talking to me. I was blanked. I walked in, said good morning and heard nothing. I realized I was in trouble and sat down at my desk in silence. I opened my laptop to find my first email of the new academic year: I had to see the head of HR – a lovely woman, one of my favourite people at the school and the mother of a guy I had gone to school with who was now a very capable host on the comedy circuit.

I headed straight to her office, went in, sat down and began to formulate all of the excuses I was going to use to get myself out of the shit. What I didn't know was that I was sewn up good and proper.

'So, I understand you couldn't come in for the exam days because Leesa was poorly?'

I nodded, for a moment believing that she had simply called me in to confirm my story and was about to send me off to enjoy the term. What an idiot.

She reached into a drawer at the bottom of her filing cabinet and pulled out a folder. She opened it on her desk and leafed through the printouts within. What she had in front of her was essentially a dossier of my Edinburgh. There were reviews, line-ups for other gigs I'd done, write-ups of various events I'd attended. There were even copies of tweets where somebody had said, 'Enjoyed your gig,' and I had replied, like the praise-hungry narcissist I am. She had even included a blog post by one of the girls I lived with during the festival.

I stayed with four girls during that Fringe, mainly because girls are much nicer to live with than boys. I even illustrated that fact by letting a mate stay in the living room for one night early on: for the next week the girls complained of a funny smell in there they couldn't get rid of. It was my friend, a pretty average-smelling bloke.

Not all girls are wonderful, though. I remember one night, at about four a.m., I was watching something on my laptop when one of the girls burst into my room, drunk, with a friend. They were after cigarettes so I joined them outside the front door for a quick smoke. Halfway through, my friend declared she needed a piss. I reminded her that our flat was furnished with two toilets, but she explained that she didn't want to go inside. She wanted to take a piss right there, whereupon she squatted by our front door and unloaded. I became concerned about getting piss on my shoes. She seemed upset that I looked distressed and said, 'Are you scared of my vagina or something? I have a beautiful vagina. Look at my vagina, Romesh. LOOK AT MY BEAUTIFUL VAGINA.' I didn't have the heart to tell her that my vagina-judgement skills were rudimentary at best.

I was at the head of HR's desk watching her leaf through all of the reviews and documents and having to process a number of things.

First, I was definitely caught. There was no way out of this. I was going to hold my hands up and accept the repercussions.

Second, who the hell put that folder together? It was meticulous enough to suggest vindictiveness, and this woman just wasn't the sort of person to try to embarrass somebody. It must have been another colleague, who had never wanted me back, and I guess this was a good way to put the boot in. I say all this as if I was upset by it but, to be honest, I understood their position: former colleague comes back and is a shit member of the team while he runs around doing comedy and faking health issues to shirk even more duties. I am clearly the prick in this situation.

Third, I was wondering whether it would be inappropriate to ask to keep the folder.

The head of HR explained that my actions had really upset the team and they felt like they couldn't work with me any more. She then said I had two options. Either go back with my tail between my legs, try to repair the damage I had done and salvage my career in the sixth form, or cut my losses and move to another head-of-year team lower down the school. I knew I couldn't go back to the sixth form as they hated me. I had also agreed with my then-agent that I would leave the job at Christmas, so it felt unfair to join another team and have them train me when I knew I was going to leave anyway. That would just be adding dick move to dick move.

I told Anne I would relinquish my head-of-year position and just be a maths teacher. This felt like the best solution. Anne, not knowing that I was planning on leaving anyway, was shocked and felt this was an extreme reaction to the situation. I assured her that I was fine with it, more than happy just to do my teaching. She said she would make the arrangements.

For the remainder of my time at Hazelwick I enjoyed myself. Not being a head of year was liberating, and I was able to gig and teach without it being too much of a strain. What made it even better was that every time I walked past a member of the sixth-form team they made a point of ignoring me. I imagine they were waiting for an apology that never came. I was too mortified to handle it. It remains one of my biggest regrets. I wish I had just sat the team down, apologized and explained my motivations. But at the time, it just felt like they wouldn't understand. Which they might not have done, but at least they would have known.

I handed in my resignation a few weeks later, which added a rose-tinted glow to my final days at work. No problem seems too large when you know that in a few weeks you won't have to worry about it. I was looking forward to starting properly as a comedian, and in the meantime we gave birth to a beautiful second son, Alex.

During my last week as a teacher, I was performing at a gig in Brighton. It was a Tuesday night and I was counting down the days to leaving Hazelwick. The gig, sadly, had been cancelled due to lack of audience, so we all decided to head over to the pub. It was there that I took a call from my brother asking me to come home straight away. When I got there, I found my family gathered around my dead father.

4.

Poppa Was a Player

My dad had died suddenly of a heart attack. My brother had come home with his wife Claire and found him dead on the sofa. I rushed back from the gig, arriving to find my distraught family standing around his body.

This was a shock at the time, but it was hardly a surprise, based on his lifestyle. My dad drank and smoked a lot, and his eating habits were aggressively unhealthy. I remember one evening he came back from a shift at the pub and decided to boil some eggs and then, bizarrely, deep fry them. He told us it was something he fancied, and we assumed he meant the eggs, but he might just as likely have meant blocked arteries.

My dad was hilarious. He was the guy who held court at parties. I have countless memories of standing in the living rooms of my parents' Sri Lankan friends and watching him, whisky in hand, deliver what essentially looked like stand-up routines. The room would be rocking. What followed afterwards was usually a lot less enjoyable. The adults would grab pots and pans, turn them upside down and use them as small drums while they drunkenly sang old Tamil songs from back in the day. It looked hilarious, and sounded like the bit in the film *Event Horizon* where you hear the noises from Hell.

My dad was a hero to me, but I know he also did some horrible things to my mum. Dad was born into a typically large Sri Lankan family. He was one of eight siblings, and Mum likes telling me that some of the other brothers fancied her too. I only have her word for that, though.

Dad came to the UK in the mid-seventies to seek his fortune. Well, initially it was to finish his accountancy exams, but he ended up staying. My family are Tamil, and things at the time were – still are – pretty awful for Tamils in Sri Lanka, so a lot of his family were eventually forced to leave their homes. I'm guessing Dad thought it was a good time to escape. Mum soon joined him and they decided to establish their life in England.

It makes me sad to think of Mum coming to the UK, because while Dad had workmates and quickly established a friendship group, Mum was essentially on her own in a foreign country with no friends or family. On top of that she was in Crawley. Which makes it all the more sad that Dad cheated on her as much as he did.

It's very difficult to write about the stuff Dad got up to because I don't want you to think ill of him. He was an absolute top bloke and a great father, and when he died he and Mum were very close, but that doesn't change the fact that he slept around, and went through a phase when he wanted to start a life with someone else.

It was a low point, but my dad later became a real rock for me. When I ran a gig at his pub, we invited him onstage and he was so good he got an encore. That might have damaged the ego of a son who was an aspiring comedian, but fortunately my anxiety and self-esteem issues have only just caught up with me, and I'm seeing a counsellor now so it's all good.

Dad was fiercely supportive of my career as a comedian, perhaps to a fault. He would often ask me why I wasn't doing *Live at the Apollo* yet, and I had to point out to him that I had only five minutes of material and nobody had heard of me. He came to as many of my gigs as he could, and got to know a lot of the comedians I gigged with: he would often be found drunkenly telling them how good they were and misquoting their material back to them. At the last gig he came to before he died, he had a few beers and was holding court with the comics, talking about the night. Then, as we were walking to my car, he asked if he'd embarrassed me. I told him he'd been hilarious and he seemed relieved.

He was in Canada visiting relatives a few months before he died and he was upset about being away because Leesa was due to give birth to Alex. When she gave birth sooner than we thought, he flew home early to meet his new grandson.

He was all about family. For his sixtieth birthday, his brothers flew to England to celebrate with him, and he was really touched. But he never quite got over the guilt of what he'd put us through. We wrote in his card that he was an amazing dad and that we looked up to him, but he refused to believe it. He kept saying he'd let us down and wouldn't accept that we loved him. I hope, deep down, he knew we did.

For the first seven years of my childhood I had a great time. We lived in a semi-detached house in Crawley, Dad drove a nice car, I went to private school and my parents bought my brother and me whatever we wanted. We were spoilt brats. I sometimes wonder whether, if we hadn't gone through what happened subsequently, we might still be brats. My kids are now where I was then, and I'm deeply paranoid about overindulging them and them not valuing what they have. I have to balance this against the desire to buy them things so they leave me in peace.

At some stage, I remember Dad starting to get wild-eyed and a bit weird. He started talking about doing deals and that if one came off we'd be millionaires. He was a Sri Lankan Del Boy. We had all sorts of new people coming round to the house and they would sit around making phone calls and saying things like 'The window is now,' and 'We need to expedite this.' These men never really spoke to anyone other than Dad, but they were very respectful and polite.

I remember Dad had gone out, and one of his 'deal buddies' was waiting on a call. I had recorded an interview with Chuck D from Public Enemy and wanted to listen to it, so went down to the living-room music system, and plugged my headphones in so I didn't disturb 'Rodney', as I began to call him. I had Chuck D in my ears and occasionally I would glance across at Rodney, who would be reading a paper or making a call.

It was about an hour into the interview when I realized I hadn't plugged the headphones in properly and had been playing the interview through the main speakers. The man had said nothing. Which means he had assumed I was such a little dick that I had decided to listen to a loud radio show even though he was at 'work', and also that I was such a lunatic I liked to wear unplugged headphones.

It became clear during this time that we had less money. I remember being super-excited about the arrival of *Apocalypse 91: The Enemy Strikes Black*, one of Public Enemy's better album titles. I asked Dad if I could buy the album and he said yes. However, when my friend came round to go to the shops with me to get it, Dad told me he couldn't afford it. I kicked off – in front of my friend, in front of Rodney, and in front of a man who looked a bit like a brown Uncle Albert. I was starting to think that the 'deal' Dad kept referring to might be an Asian *Only Fools and Horses* remake.

Dad looked crestfallen. He asked Rodney if he could borrow the money, Rodney agreed, and Dad gave the money to his ungrateful little shit of a son so he could buy an album. That is one of my worst memories of time with Dad, and I never got to apologize to him for it. I know I'd react differently if one of my kids threw that tantrum but I wonder how much of that is down to recognizing how ugly that attitude was in me. I'd do anything to stamp it out in my own children.

It started to become more apparent that Dad was struggling. Money was tighter, and there was a lot more cash about, which I learned to be a sign that we were living hand to mouth. Mum and Dad stopped buying things and the cupboards were looking a touch post-apocalyptic. Then one day they sat us down and told us we were moving.

My brother and I were gutted. We didn't want to leave our house, particularly as we were moving from a rather nice part of Crawley to what was notoriously its roughest borough, but even at that age, spoiled Romesh and Dinesh knew that Dad was in a bad way. So we pretended we were excited, and began to pack up our things.

Our house was being repossessed so we moved into a place that was rented to us by one of Mum and Dad's friends. It was a nice, modest little house, but we were all sad to be leaving behind the privileges we'd enjoyed for so long.

Then Dad seemed to disappear. There was no announcement, but suddenly he had to work lots and that work often kept him away overnight. Mum was very matter-of-fact about it, but essentially she was shepherding us through this period of upheaval on her own.

One morning a friend of hers came to the house to look after us and Mum said she had to pop out. She booked a taxi and headed off to 'deal with something'.

She had discovered that Dad was having an ongoing affair with the wife of one of the couples they hung out with. Mum had started to suspect that was where Dad was going and had decided to confront them. I have no idea what she was hoping to achieve by doorstepping them, but she has since told me what happened. She saw them through the window behaving like a couple in love, and banged on the door. She says she just wanted to challenge them. What she didn't expect was for Dad to show no remorse at all. In fact, he seemed relieved that the encounter took him one step closer to a life without us. I can't imagine what that was like for her to go through.

I have tried many times to put myself in Dad's position in all of this, because he was such a loving man, but from any angle this was pretty unforgivable behaviour. Having tried and failed to keep us afloat, his intention was, I believe, to offload us into a council property and have a relationship with the other woman. So, a young girl had come all the way to England from Sri Lanka to be with my father, she had given birth to his two children, raised them and stood by him through the good and increasingly bad times, and he was now trying to get rid of her.

Mum was obviously shocked at Dad's stubborn indifference, and things only got worse. We had to move out of the rented house and applied for council housing. Nothing was available immediately, so we were temporarily housed in a bed-and-breakfast. Dad was still absent as he was spending time at his new lover's house. I wish I could have helped Mum through this period, but I'm ashamed to say that my instinct was to confect a fantasy in which I decided she must be mistaken and that Dad really was just away at work. A coping mechanism, I suppose.

It was a pretty rough time. Mum, my brother and I were all sleeping in the same room and I used to hear Mum crying long into the night. I'd say it was hard to listen to, but in fact I was numb to the situation. I was in shock. Just six months previously we had been a traditional family unit in a lovely house with nice holidays and all the comforts of what felt like a normal childhood. Now Dad was shacked up with another woman and we were in a B-and-B. Having seen my mum go through that, and still have the strength to bring us up, I know I can never repay my debt to her. Based on the birthday presents she asks for, she seems to agree. Most people, when asked what they want, will suggest something small or nothing at all. My mum will say, 'A MacBook' or 'An iPad' or 'A house.' And then she'll shoot me a look as if to say, 'Remember the B-and-B?'

I remember starting year ten, and after a history lesson, my teacher walking up to me and saying he'd heard I wasn't going to be at the school any more. I denied it, partly because he had asked me in front of friends but mostly because I didn't know what he was talking about. However, the fact my parents were struggling meant I figured out there was some issue with fee payment. I assume Dad did what most people do when they owe money, which is stop answering calls and ignore letters. This meant that I became the school's only means of communication with my parents: I would be sitting in a maths lesson and someone would come in and hand me a final-demand letter. In my bag was every single letter they had ever given me to pass to my parents, from my very first day there. For the school to imagine that I, one of its most disorganized students, would be more reliable than the postal service was foolish.

By now I had attended Reigate Grammar School for a few years, having won a scholarship on account of my being a genius. That is one opinion. The other is that my parents paid for me to be privately tutored to the eyeballs, to the point at which I was penning scholarship-winning essays in my sleep. The training was intense, and by the age of ten I was ready to take entrance exams for two schools: Sevenoaks and Reigate Grammar. I clearly remember my mum and dad dropping me off at the exam venue and me being utterly terrified. My mum later told me that my dad had seen the distraught look on my face as I was walking into the exam hall and had had a little cry. So, screw you, he was a lovely man.

I was an extremely nervous exam taker. I combined this with a complete lack of work ethic or preparation – despite all the personal tutoring. Every one of my reports says, 'Lazy' or 'Does not meet potential' or 'Does not seem to care'. As a student I did little or no work, then became intensely worried about how I would do in exams, and angry when things didn't go my way.

That didn't end at school. Years later I ended up doing an economics degree. There was a module on econometrics, which I found impenetrable. I made it through the exam by memorizing entire solutions, then looked for the triggers in the questions to see what was being asked, and vomited out answers of which I had absolutely zero comprehension. I ended up with a 2:1 in that module. A girl I had been in class with that year could not have been more appalled: she slightly lost her temper, claiming there was no way I knew enough even to pass the exam. I can now admit here that she was correct.

The Gods of Econometrics were to have their revenge when I was studying for my master's degree in the same subject – having tried to stretch out my student years for as long as possible. We were living on a council estate at the time, and I decided to do an all-nighter to prepare for the exam the next day. This meant buying a packet of cigarettes and a lot of 'Rocket Fuel' – strong instant coffee that students often drank in my day when they wanted to meet deadlines. You would basically have one cup of it, then spend the evening worried that your heart was going to explode. It was incredible.

At about three in the morning I'd just got my head around the econometrics, when there was a knock on the door. It was one of our neighbours, a man I'd long suspected was a bit of a prick. In fact, years later, my wife and I moved back into that house and he was still living on the street. He approached me one day and asked me if I was happy with my headlights. I replied that I was. He hadn't much small-talk. He then told me he had some better bulbs that would fit my car, which he would give me for ten pounds. I agreed, mainly to bring the conversation to as swift an end as possible, but asked if he could wait for me to deliver the money – which I had no intention of doing – before giving me the bulbs.

He was determined to make the sale, though, and when I returned home later that day, Leesa told me he'd dropped them off. Two days later, I returned from a gig to find a note through the letterbox from our light-bulb-dealing neighbour. It read: 'Romesh, I think it's better if you return the bulbs to me as soon as possible, to avoid any further awkwardness.' What a tosser. I bundled them together and returned them with a note explaining I hadn't wanted them in the first place. For the two years I continued to live there he refused to speak to me. Over some headlight bulbs. That's what you'd call a result.

It wasn't the only run-in we had with the neighbours in that street. One of the women living there became obsessed with my wife's parking – or, rather, my parking, which she assumed was my wife's. It began with her speaking to me one day about our car being crooked, complaining about Leesa being inconsiderate. It was incredibly tempting to agree with her and start slating my wife's driving but I knew that if Leesa found out I'd done that, even for a laugh, she would turn my nuts into a smooth paste. So I simply told the woman I'd have a word with my reckless parker of a wife.

Two weeks later, I was about to go into a gig, and was desperate for the toilet, when I received a phone call from Leesa. She was furious. She'd had a note through the door from the woman in question saying that Leesa had once again parked erroneously and was displaying a 'lack of consideration for the street'. She had 'discussed it with the neighbours and some of them felt the same'. Now I was faced with a difficult situation: Leesa wanted to go straight over to the woman's house and punch her in the face. I had to calm her down quickly: I didn't want her to start a war, and I was desperate for a poo.

I'm slightly loath to tell the next part of the story because Flo, my agent, keeps telling me that I have way too many stories about toilet situations going wrong, but my life is plagued by them. The number of times I've been desperate for a piss and/or poo with an approaching emergency status is higher for me than anyone else on the planet. I'm like a kid: in an instant I go from not needing the loo to being side-splittingly desperate. I haven't adjusted to it.

I managed to calm Leesa down and get off the phone, whereupon I penguin-strutted into the comedy venue to ask where the toilet was. They informed me that the men's were out of order but I could use the ladies'. Ordinarily, I might try to find another venue, but we were beyond emergency territory now. So I ran into the first cubicle. At that point I heard the door swing open and three women walked in, chatting and laughing. This was slightly alarming: I'd have to stay in the cubicle until they left. It was also slightly exhilarating – in a non-pervy way – as I was actually party to a girly toilet conversation. They were chatting about work and how somebody was a twat and I was quite enjoying myself when one of them banged on the door and asked if there was any spare toilet tissue in my cubicle.

It was at this point I became worried. I started to assess my options. I could either answer, then have to explain what I was doing there and that they should stop screaming. Or I could avoid that by silently passing some tissue out. This was a tempting option until it occurred to me that she might see enough of my hand to ascertain it was a man, in which case I would be a man sitting silently in a women's toilet. I identified a third option, which I took, which was to do absolutely nothing. She knocked on the door again and asked the question once more. I remained silent. It was agonizing. She did it one more time, then called me a bitch. After that they were quiet, probably mouthing to each other what an ignorant cow I was, then eventually they left.

I had aggravated that woman, and now I was concerned that she might be waiting outside for me to find out who had blanked her. I couldn't see how discovering I was a man would make the situation any less awkward so I was faced with another tricky situation. I was either going to be set upon or reported as a weirdo. If the latter, I'd have to take them to the bar to find the guy who told me to use the ladies', but I was sure he'd have disappeared and I'd have to spend the rest of my life as a registered sex offender.

I could ascertain only one realistic way out. Wait there long enough for them either to get bored or to assume there was nobody in my cubicle – it was locked because it was out of order and some size-eleven Converse had been placed on the floor as decoration. I couldn't wander around the toilet as I'd risk another woman walking in and all of a sudden I'd be a serial offender.

I stayed in that cubicle for an hour.

So it's three in the morning, I'm revising for my econometrics exam, and my neighbour has knocked on my door. I opened it with all the relish you might muster if you knew that in fifteen years you were going to have an argument with the man over headlights. He was out of breath and flustered: 'Somebody's just smashed into your car and is still driving around the street like a maniac.'

There are some things you wish you were there for so you could stop them happening. Maybe you could catch a burglar in the act, or you could have been at a work meeting and intervened before a terrible decision was made. This was one of the situations where I would happily have discovered the aftermath in the morning. I wasn't sure what he expected me to do. Did he want me to tackle the guy? I asked.

'I don't fucking know! Just get out there!'

I shouted for my brother and we grabbed cricket bats, which felt like the right thing to do, then ran outside. We discovered a guy off his tits in what was clearly a stolen car just pinballing around the estate car park. I figured out that my neighbour wanted to stop this but not to deal with it himself so used our damaged car as leverage to secure himself two servants.

In a far less exciting face-off than you might think, we managed to corner the man and call the police, then wait for them. Once they'd been, arrested the guy and taken our statements, Mum asked me to sort out the insurance, insisting I call the company immediately. By the time I got off the phone it was five thirty a.m. and I had a couple of hours before I had to leave for my exam, having lost about 20 per cent of my total revision time.

Frazzled by the experience, I smashed down some more caffeine and headed to uni, meeting up with my girlfriend, who was on the same course. We were chatting about the exam as we headed into London on the train and I started to feel increasingly confident of giving a good account of myself. By the time we arrived I was excited about how I was going to get on. We filed into the hall, took our seats and were told to start.

It was upon opening the exam paper that it slowly dawned on me that I really didn't have a fucking clue about econometrics. Not just that: it soon became clear that not only was I unsure of the answers, but I could not discern what the questions were asking me. For forty-five minutes I stared at them, trying to decipher them, to no avail. I then spent fifteen minutes trying not to cry. I still had two hours left. I spent those two hours doing absolutely nothing. I couldn't answer anything, but I didn't want to leave as everybody looked very busy and I didn't want to draw attention to myself.

As the end of the allotted time approached, I started to feel bad that I had not managed to internalize any of the course. I felt guilty about the money I had spent on tuition fees, and I felt bad for the lecturer who had seemed pretty good. (He might not have been amazing: he had in me a student who had sat through his classes and retained nothing, but I still felt bad.) To try to alleviate this, just before the exam finished I wrote, 'I am very sorry,' on my answer sheet. I remember talking to friends on the way out and they were all saying how hard the paper was and how they would have to lower the grade boundaries. My only hope was that you could achieve a pass mark by correctly spelling Ranganathan.

My exam experiences have influenced my parenting style. My eldest son is nine and is constantly worried about homework, tests and being top of his class. I find this quite upsetting. Life is so full of challenges, and working hard, disappointment and stress that I'm really keen for our children not to experience any of it. In year two, he did his Key Stage 1 exams and I was struck by how many parents were getting their kids to do practice papers and extra revision, with some even hiring tutors. While I understand this strategy for teenagers, I don't understand trying to inflate the attainment level of such young kids. They're at the level they're at. If they over-perform in an exam, they're only going to be out of sync with their peers. Also, life's too fucking short, isn't it?

All of which begs the question, 'How much more can you possibly digress from a story about your father?'

We had been in the B-and-B for a while when my mum

became concerned that we hadn't heard from Dad for a couple of days. She couldn't get hold of him and decided that the best course of action was to head once again to his lover's house.

When we pulled up, we couldn't see any sign of my dad, so Mum went to the door and demanded to know his whereabouts. The woman explained Dad had been there until two days previously, when he had gone off to do 'a deal', had been raided by the police and was now in prison.

We soon discovered that all of these deals he had been involved in were highly illegal and the police had been surveilling him and his associates for a while. They had busted them and arrested Dad. The Asian *Only Fools and Horses* remake had taken a dark turn.

This was a proper sucker punch to the family. My dad was sentenced to two years for fraud. He was moved to Ford open prison in West Sussex, and we spent our Sundays travelling to see him. It felt properly grimy, but every now and again he was allowed to come home with us for the day. That blew my mind. As a kid, I couldn't understand why the prison let him come home and trusted him not to do a bunk. As if he would rather spend a life on the run, trying to avoid driving through Ford, than just serve the rest of his short sentence. After he passed away, Mum told me he didn't want us to know that he'd had some horrible experiences inside, including being beaten up by another prisoner one lunchtime. But he also told me that he'd tried weed for the first time in there, so it must have been swings and roundabouts.

Weirdly, Dad going to prison turned out to be the best

thing that could have happened to the family. He suddenly realized he had let us all down and wanted to make it up to us. He reconciled with Mum, binned off the girlfriend and became a loving husband and father again.

I remember being reluctant to welcome Dad back straight away. One night, I had been out late without having bothered to tell anyone where I was. When I arrived home, Dad was annoyed. He had a go at me for my lack of consideration. I did something I have regretted ever since. I turned on him. I asked him what business he had telling me anything when he had been so ready to get rid of us. I told him he had no right to tell me what to do. And I told him he hadn't been a real dad. He said nothing. He just sat and accepted everything I said to him. I finished my rant and stormed out. He looked so sad.

The two of us never spoke about that night. After he died, I remember a deep sadness that I had never apologized to him for the way I'd spoken to him, and the things I'd said. Although we were all very close by the time he passed away, he had never overcome the guilt he felt at letting us down, and I couldn't help but feel I had contributed to that.

Dad was a wonderful man – funnier and more loving than I'll ever be – but his actions made me vow that I would never let people down as he had. A promise I have consistently failed to keep.

5.

Every Day I'm Hustling

The reason I went into teaching was a small bout of depression, which, ironically, is one of the main reasons people leave the profession. Depression feels like a heavy label for what I experienced, but I was in a bad place, suffering from anxiety about where my life was headed. I was working as a cost analyst for an airline catering company, LSG Sky Chefs. It meant telling airlines how much we would charge them for the food they were ordering for their planes. If they wanted an extra tomato on their economy salad I would have to charge them for the tomatoes, the cost of someone putting them there and of me figuring it all out. The description of the job I've just given you is more entertaining and life-affirming than anything I encountered during the entirety of my time working there.

I found the job unacceptable eventually, mainly because it combined incredibly long hours with an industry in which I had no interest. I'm not suggesting the job was a true calling for any of my colleagues, that one day they were on a flight, tried a meal that tasted like sautéed effluent, and thought, I'm going to make this my life's work. But I've realized that I can only work hard when I'm enthused by what I'm doing. I know that's entitlement at its worst, and a privileged attitude when so many people have to work long hours at jobs they hate just to survive.

When my parents were broke and I was doing A levels I decided I needed a job to get by, not because I had to put food on the table but because at seventeen you want to buy weed and Armani T-shirts to impress girls, and my parents couldn't get me either of those essentials. So I started applying for jobs. I already had some solid work experience from a stint at KFC in Crawley, but those days were behind me, mainly because working at KFC as a vegetarian seemed morally corrupt. And I was sick of having to eat chip butties and corn on the cob for lunch every day.

Until recently, Nando's did an amazing veggie burger – a soy and tomato thing, which sounds horrible but you'll just have to trust me. I really cannot imagine somebody reading this who eats meat is thinking, *Soy and tomato? Why the hell am I eating beef burgers?* It's nice, dickhead. Anyway, they've changed it now and the burgers aren't vegan any more so I'm done. But it does beg the question as to why the hell a vegan has any business eating in a Nando's, veggie options or not. The core business of Nando's is killing chickens and I'm supporting that by eating there. It makes no sense. There's a chicken in the bloody logo. You can't support something you fundamentally disagree with because it has one thing you like. It's like visiting Piers Morgan's house because he has nice coffee.

I did start to get worried that being vegan had meant my taste-buds had become 'veganized' – that I'd become convinced crap things are tasty. I knew a little bit of taste-bud training was going on because when I first went veggie

74

I still craved meat. Now the idea of eating meat feels pretty rank. However, I do also see lots of things that are advertised as 'vegan and delicious', and I'm comforted by the fact they still look and taste like somebody grated a tree.

I invited Seann Walsh and his girlfriend to our house for dinner once, and I cooked them a three-course vegan feast. The dessert was a recipe I had googled after trying an amazing chocolate mousse that was comprised almost entirely of avocado. The recipe I used said, 'Your guests will not be able to tell the difference!' I whipped up the mousse, tried it and nearly wrote an email to the recipe writer to thank them for that heavenly delight. I then spent the evening incredibly excited about our guests tasting it. I almost didn't care if they enjoyed the first two courses as I had this dynamite pudding. The time came, I put on some music to welcome the *pièce de résistance* to the table, and then I served the mousse. There was silence as they started to eat. I ate mine and thought, Romesh you absolute don – you've smashed this. My next thought was interrupted by Seann asking me why I would put vegetables in a dessert. Everyone else at the table pissed themselves laughing and it occurred to me I hadn't eaten a regular chocolate mousse for years. It turns out that the recipe tagline should have been 'Your guests won't be able to tell the difference between this and shit in a bowl.'

I used to do the late shifts on a Friday and Saturday night at KFC, during my GCSE years, which made me a Wetherspoons post-traumatic stress counsellor. Essentially I spent my entire shift dealing with post-pub knobheads. The staff were almost exclusively Sri Lankan, mainly because of Sri Lanka's deep connections with the fried-chicken culture of southern America. I don't want to cast aspersions but a raid on that branch of KFC would have uncovered eleven herbs and spices and twelve possible cases for deportation. I met more Sri Lankans there than on the first series of *Asian Provocateur*.

I was on the take, not money wise, but mates used to come in and order a portion of fries and I would sort them out with some freebies. Unfortunately mates would tell other mates and then I'd get people I barely knew coming in and expecting handouts. I realized things were out of control when at the end of one night the manager asked me why we were sixty Hot Wings short. I don't think it would have been acceptable to say, 'Because a group of lads I'm scared of from school came in after smoking a lot of weed.'

There were lots of pranks at KFC. You couldn't leave a drink anywhere without some dick putting mayo or salt in it, which was irritating and a damning indictment of what passes for banter at a fast-food place. There was a man called Fazal, a friend of the family, who loved asking me to pass him something, and when I bent down to get it, he would fart in my face. In a food shop. Nice one. He was also a fry thief. Ordinarily when you took an order with fries, you would bag up the fries, leave them in the rack, then go to get the chicken. Fazal didn't do that. He would get the chicken, then take your fries for his order. That doesn't sound like a big deal, but when we were serving the post-pub rush, I could have happily bludgeoned him to death every time he did it. I'm getting angry about it even now. He was a lovely man, but his fries policy was abhorrent and for that reason I hope he never finds happiness.

Just as I'd had enough of KFC, Sainsbury's were opening a branch down the road in Horsham and were looking for loads of staff. I applied to them. When I turned up to the interview, the woman looked at me with concern.

'Is your eye okay?'

'Er, yes, it's just something I've had since I was a kid.'

'Oh, right. Well, sit down.'

Now, I don't know if this woman had some sort of past as an eye specialist, but from then on all she could do was tell me how I should probably get it sorted out and how easy it would be to have surgery. Every single question somehow led back to my eye. You might think this would upset me, but I was delighted: the woman was talking to me with real sympathy in her voice, which meant she felt sorry for me because of my 'affliction', which meant she was almost definitely going to give me a job, unless she found me so hideously unattractive that she wouldn't want me anywhere near customers.

Having a lazy eye has been a weird one. I had a horrible infection when I was three, which left me with the lazy eye and a droopy eyelid. I think my mum was worried about surgery and I guess she thought it might be hard at school if I didn't get bullied or if girls thought I was attractive. Ever since, my eye has been a physical interpretation of my character. I genuinely don't think I would have been a comedian if I hadn't had it. I was fat, which helps with the development of a comedic persona, but that combined with the lazy eye meant that I had to come up with a sophisticated set of systems to defend myself at school. It also means I have the same field of vision as a barn owl.

Being on social media has taken me back to my school-days because people are vile. Individuals are wonderful and lovely and great, but people as a collective are the worst. I get so many hateful comments about my lazy eye now. I recently received a tweet from somebody saying, 'I saw your lazy eye and it made me want to throw up.' Unimaginative, but I admire the brutality of the diss. I retweeted it, saying, 'Don't normally retweet praise but . . .' which felt like the high road. I sat back and waited to be declared King of Twitter.

I looked at this guy's profile and it was just full of him saying the most horrible things to people he'd seen on television. And then, while I was looking at it, another tweet popped up: 'Oh my God, I am absolutely shaking with excitement.' And then I saw replies from his friends going, 'You got another one, you legend,' and 'I can't believe you did it! Amazing.' He saw me retweeting his insult as a victory. Then I realized that even if you've got a good response, it's never going to be as effective as just ignoring it. I imagine that if he sees it's been included in this book, his head will explode. I hope it helps him lose his virginity.

I remember being upset the first couple of times I got negative comments but my skin is a little thicker now. I did report it, though, when someone really crossed a line. On an early *Mock the Week*, I observed that old people should be allowed to be racist because they have enough going on. I thought nothing of it. The day after the show went out, I got a message saying something along the lines of 'Saw what you said about old people on *Mock the Week*. My grandparents didn't fight in the war so that Pakis like you could express your views. If I ever found out where you lived I would end your worthless life.' I don't recall ever claiming that his grandparents fought in the war so I could do *Mock the Week*, but I could confidently argue that they didn't fight in the war so that losers could type abuse at people from the comfort of their bedrooms.

I reported it to the police, not because I thought it was a credible threat but because people shouldn't be able to spout off shit like that without repercussions. Also the guy had posted it to my website, which requires you to put in your email address to leave a message, so it wasn't as anonymous as he'd perhaps assumed.

The police were amazing. They took it seriously and got a full statement from me, then said they'd find this person and take action. They kept me fully updated all the way. They eventually located the guy's house and spoke to him. Apparently he couldn't believe the message had been traced back to his address. He was so scared that the police told me it was probably overkill to press charges, and asked if I would be satisfied with a letter of apology. I said that would be fine. If anything it would be nice to receive a letter.

A couple of days later I received a letter that painted a picture of a very different man from the one who'd sent a death threat to someone he'd never met. The letter said this person had been drinking wine while watching Second World War documentaries and was getting very worked up about history. He'd switched to BBC2, found me talking about old people and become enraged. He sent me an angry message. It all seemed a bit sad. But I still think he's not a great guy. Nobody goes, 'Isn't it a nightmare when you have a touch too much Chablis, then issue a death threat to a Paki?'

My intuition about the Sainsbury's interviewer's pro-disability bias was right and I was offered a job at the shiny new store in Horsham, alongside probably every teenager in West Sussex. I went along to training where we were all allocated jobs. I had made the decision that I wanted to be on trolleys. It seemed like the perfect choice. I didn't have to deal with customers, I didn't have to talk to anyone, and everybody hated that job so it would look like I was being really noble. Perfect. They were more than happy to let me do it, but they did offer to till-train me so that I could operate the checkout if I ever wanted to transfer to that job. I declined. I knew what that meant: if they got super-busy or someone called in sick I'd have to go in and get on a till. No thanks, mate.

I ended up having to work at Sainsbury's a lot, as I was doing A-level Spanish, which involved an exchange trip my parents couldn't afford. I was there almost every night until I'd paid off the school. Initially I was very keen, and would work as quickly as possible, lashing loads of trolleys together to try to keep the car park as free of them as I could. It was a hell of a job when you were keen. You'd start to see it as a game. You'd work out the best routes to take, while avoiding cars and negotiating chicanes in the parking bays, to get the trolleys back as painlessly as possible. I remember one day I managed to navigate thirty-five trolleys in one chain back to the store from the opposite side of the car park. That's not something just anybody can do.

Gradually I started to lose enthusiasm: I realized that the trolley wallies were bottom of the food chain. One day it was raining and the management decided they didn't want customers to get their arms wet when reaching for tickets at the car park barrier. I was therefore tasked with standing at the ticket machine and passing them to the customers as they drove by. Awful. So awful, in fact, that customers were laughing and joking with me about how crap my job was. I tackled the boredom by talking to them in as many different accents as I could manage. I started with one that I didn't think would alert any suspicion – generic Asian – then moved on to Irish, Welsh, Australian and American. I am pretty sure I even smashed out a Chinese voice. I discovered it takes a really ballsy person to say, 'I'm sorry but I don't think that's how you really speak', particularly when you're an Asian-looking English-speaking guy with a lazy eye.

I realized I had to leave the job when I was just looking for ways to get through the shift. I would occasionally start by hiding one of the trolleys in the nearby park, then go to my manager and tell them that a customer had spotted a rogue trolley, at which point I would be asked to go and get it. I would then spend as long as possible wandering around the park until I eventually 'found' said trolley and could return it as slowly as possible. I was occasionally asked to help out in the store – not on checkout, obviously – and discovered that if I walked around with a basket with some items in it, people would assume I was working, returning stock to shelves. Whole shifts would pass like that. Eventually my time-wasting started to feel like I was stealing from the company. Which I was doing literally as well. Most of my nineties R&B collection is from Horsham Sainsbury's.

I'm really into hip hop (if you don't know that about me, I'm slightly disappointed), and I would find as many opportunities to listen to as much of it as possible all the time. I used to get a Sainsbury's coat, put the hood up and plug in earphones so that I could listen to music throughout my shift. I did it regardless of the weather so I must have looked mental. Now I strongly associate that period of my life with the music I was listening to at the time, which means I can't listen to anything by Ice Cube without thinking of a supermarket. The earphones also meant that I couldn't hear any traffic, which wasn't ideal when I was working in a car park. I remember once pulling some trolleys out of a bay backwards, falling onto and rolling over the bonnet of a customer's car because I hadn't heard it approach. I fell to the ground, stood up, pulled my hood back on and walked away with the trolleys, like Iron Man walking away from an explosion. As it turned out, I was supposed to check the customer's car for any possible damage.

Anyway, I'd moved up the ladder since those days at the supermarket, but I was finding my job at LSG Sky Chefs really tough. It was really hard, both technically and in terms of the hours. I find it incredibly difficult to be good at things I care about, so not caring about something makes it a lot harder. One of the accounts I was looking after was Air New Zealand's. I can tell you now that Air New Zealand is amazing. I worked with a lot of airlines and Air New Zealand seemed to care the most: they would taste and examine the vegan and kosher meals while most other airlines would be happy with whatever you found knocking about. This, however, made their account difficult to look after as they were so meticulous, scrutinizing the ingredients and every last detail.

I remember that a deadline was approaching and I kept screwing it up, so I went upstairs to the toilet for what I thought was a wee. But when I got there, I went into one of the cubicles, sat down and cried. I don't know what triggered it, but maybe I was stressed and depressed in a job I thought I'd be stuck in for life. It didn't help that everybody else in the office seemed as miserable as I was, but had been working there for years, which meant I was starting to think that all work was awful and that was just how life is.

I feel somewhat embarrassed writing this now, because I know that horrible jobs are a reality for many people. I get it. But the physical difference between me doing a job that my heart isn't in and one that I love is vast. I guess that's why I continued to try to do comedy even though for many years I was running close to a loss, and all the signs were telling me I should give up and return to a nine-to-five.

One of the other things I discovered about working in an office was that sexual politics were rife. A week wouldn't pass without somebody shagging somebody else and it being the talk of the office. We would even get news of what was going on at the other offices across the country. It was quite the little soap opera.

I remember being pretty naïve about this. I went along to a work drinks one night and it was all going swimmingly. Everyone was starting to get drunk and telling each other they loved them or talking about who they fancied. A woman came stumbling over to me for a chat. She was one of those 'life and soul of the office' types and often had a funny anecdote that would take your mind off the mundanity of the job. Maybe that's who I should have been, since I went on to become a comedian but, no, I was the guy who cried in the toilet. She came over and sat on my lap, and as we were talking, her hand moved around me. Next thing, she was gripping me up. Initially I wasn't sure, because I hadn't had any real experience of pulling. And you can never be sure of someone's intentions. What I didn't think was accidental was her stroking my penis. The weird thing was, because she was such a joker, because both of us were in relationships and because I had no clue about women, I assumed she was playing a prank: I jumped up and went, 'Ha-ha-ha! She was pretending to try it on with me! She properly groped me!' I looked at her face and she was mortified. Sleeping with her felt like the politest option. I'm joking. It wasn't polite, it was raw and dirty. I'm joking. We didn't have sex.

Back to toilet-crying: I'd just had my first. I returned to my desk and felt loads better. It was like I'd pressed the reset button and was ready to carry on with work. For a couple of months that became my coping strategy. Every so often, I'd feel the stress or sadness mounting and would wander up to the toilet to have a little cry.

After a few weeks of this, I decided it was not a way to live my life and started to explore other options. I'd always wanted to give teaching a go, partly because my own experiences in education had been so strongly affected by negative and positive teachers.

I once had a maths teacher at Reigate Grammar School who was so scary that I started pretending I was ill just to avoid him. He would scowl and stride around the classroom barking at anyone, but I felt he had a particular dislike for me. He probably didn't, but if a child thinks you have a problem with them or that you dislike them, you're doing something wrong. I remember him teaching us equations. He started the lesson by giving us a problem to solve. The next day we started his lesson in the same way, but I noticed that the problem was identical to the one the day before. I raised my hand.

'What is it?'

'Sir, I think this problem is the same one as the one we did yesterday?'

'There is an orifice in the middle of your face, Ranganathan, and it's too big – shut it.'

Now it's possible that I have misremembered how I said what I said. I might have said, 'Oi, dickhead, why are you giving us the same problem as yesterday?' It's unlikely. What is definitely accurate is his response. It's burned into my memory. I can remember his face as he said it. And that is one of the experiences I often drew on when I went into teaching. First, because, among others, it led me to feign sickness for many of my maths lessons that year but also because it was so unfair. I had spotted what I thought was an error, and wanted to point it out to the teacher. He had rewarded me by shouting.

I didn't want to go back to university so that was a stumbling block. Then I read about a graduate teacher programme that aimed to bring more people to the profession: you were placed at a school and trained on the job, working up your skills and occasionally taking classes. This felt perfect for me, but I hesitated when I saw that the nearest place to me that ran the scheme was Hazelwick School, where I'd gone as a student. Nevertheless, I was desperate to get out of my job and the opportunity seemed too perfect, so I phoned them. They told me they were starting a new programme in a week or so and asked if I could come in for a chat in the next couple of days. I turned up, spoke to them, and they offered me a place on the course, which I immediately accepted. I quit my job at LSG the same day, and a week later I was a trainee teacher.

It was very strange walking back into Hazelwick as a trainee at twenty-three because so many people who had taught me were still there. Seeing them as colleagues was a whole new experience, and I was shocked to discover that they were actually normal people with normal lives, who breathed, ate and slept like you or I. I had no idea this was the case when I was at school, seeing them through the teacher–student divide.

Margaret Salter had been at the school for about thirty years. When I was a student she had a reputation for being terrifying but effective. It took me five minutes of speaking to her as an adult to realize that she was one of the loveliest people you could ever hope to meet. I was asked to watch one of her lessons to observe her behaviour management. As we were walking in, she warned me that this was one of her most challenging classes. I readied myself to see the mighty Margaret Salter in action, but the class had already handed out the books before her arrival and were waiting to start the lesson. The kids spent the hour engaged and behaving immaculately. I became immediately intrigued by what her idea of a good class might look like. I assume they participated in the lesson while washing her car or giving her a foot rub.

The children I would end up teaching never gave me such an easy ride, but the lessons I learned as a teacher on behaviour management I have carried with me into parenting. For example, we were told that if a kid is acting up, it's better to say, 'Your behaviour is causing a problem here,' than 'You are causing a problem here,' because it distances the child from the behaviour. It shows that you are annoyed with what they're doing rather than with them as a person. I think that's the science behind it. It makes a noticeable difference, and has helped control our three sons, who seem intent on turning our house into a zoo.

There is a belief among some people who watch my stand-up that I hate my kids, or at least one of them, and that I hate other people's kids too. This is all true. Seriously, though, it's one of the things I worry about most from what I talk about onstage.

At the end of 2017, my tour show *Irrational* was shown on

BBC2. It includes a routine about how my first child is an angel and my second son is the opposite. Just after that show went on TV, somebody messaged me: *You are a disgusting excuse for a parent, I hope your son burns your house down when he grows up*, or something to that effect. Now, this person is obviously batshit, but I was still concerned by what they said.

I have discussed this with other comedians, and many of them won't talk about their children onstage because they don't 'own those stories'. Indeed, my children didn't sign up to provide me with material, so maybe they shouldn't have to suffer their lives being plundered for my amusement. On the other hand, they want Xbox games so they're going to have to deal with it.

I did an interview once for the *Mirror*, and they supplemented what I said with lines from my stand-up as if I had used them in conversation. Stand-up, or certainly my stand-up, always looks harsher when it's written down. Then they took one of those lines and made it into the headline for the story: *Romesh Ranganathan explains why he regrets having three children*. Bloody hell. Imagine your kids reading that. I can't complain, though, because I do say that in my stand-up, but I hope it's obvious that I don't mean it. I mean, three kids are too many by any reasonable standard, but I love having them and certainly don't regret anything about it. And it certainly feels lucky to have rolled the genetic dice three times and have them all look like their mum.

The stand-up I do about my children shocks some people, and I do get a few gasps, because I'm saying what parents are not supposed to say about their kids. People laugh because it's all relatable – but not socially acceptable to say out loud. In one of my gigs I say of my second son, 'What a prick this kid is. I love him but I don't like him.' I love my second son, obviously, and I'm hoping my audience understands that what I'm really saying is: 'I adore my kids, but this is how they make me feel sometimes.' Clearly not everybody interprets it that way, because some people think I really hate my second son. And that is sad. But it's not my responsibility. I love my kids and that's it. But the second one can be a prick.

My jokes are jokes. But they come from honesty and real experience. Sometimes I wonder if my children, who have all come under the cosh of my routines, will grow up, see what I've said and decide they don't like a dad who says that kind of stuff for other people's amusement onstage. I hope our parenting enables our children to understand that we love them very much, and if they have an issue with my material I guess I'll have to accept that. And offer to pay for their counselling.

I also have to accept that I don't have a clue how to bring up my children, which is ironic given what you've been reading about my teaching days. It's proving to be a nightmare. When we had our first kid, we read all of these books about how to get them sleeping through the night, how to encourage their development, how as they get older you should give them options and make them feel part of the process, blah-blah. And it worked. I would calmly explain to Theo that his behaviour was a problem and if he carried on like that he would have to face a consequence. He would give his opinion and we would arrive at a happy resolution. Our second son, Alex, couldn't care less. You present him with options and he says no to both. And then he presents you with his option that makes you lose your shit.

Weirdly, I don't worry about him that much, not because I don't care: he's so spirited that he won't have problems as an adult. It's like having a rock star in the house: 'I don't want Cheerios, nooooo!' he shouts, as he tips over the bowl. Our youngest, Charlie, is from the same mould, so in terms of well-behaved kids we are one for three.

I do find it surprising and counter-intuitive that people are put under so much pressure to have children. Couples who don't are asked if there's a problem, and are seen as selfish if they have no plans to start a family. I wonder if the default setting should change so that it's accepted there'll be no kids, until you work out whether or not to have them. That doesn't take into account the number of people crossing their fingers and using the withdrawal method, but the big decision should be to *have* kids, not the other way round. People say, 'They've decided not to have kids,' but that shouldn't be the decision. There are so many challenges to bringing up children, and I spend most days wondering if Leesa and I are up to them.

You are defined by your childhood. After what happened with my parents I became terrified of finance and my marriage failing. But it goes much deeper than that. When I was a little kid my mum would see me in my pants or swim shorts and say, 'Look at your boobies.' Which was funny, because my mum has the perfect accent for saying 'boobies' – it's hilarious.

Ever since then, although it's possible the two things are unrelated, I've had massive issues regarding my body.

I've struggled with my weight and body image, and have been reluctant to go swimming because I didn't want to take my top off. I was once out with Leesa and the kids in LA wearing a new T-shirt (a Notorious BIG one, because I'm a don) and we walked past a shop window when I saw how fat I looked in it. I discussed with Leesa whether or not we could go home. She talked me off the ledge, and I vowed never again to wear that T-shirt in public.

The point is, how the hell can you be trusted not to give your child a major hang-up? Leesa and I are constantly disagreeing about it. For example, our children have just received their school reports. Our eldest's are always amazing, and we congratulate him on how well he's done. The subjects are graded either 'needs development', which means needs more work to achieve the appropriate level at their age, 'at expected level' or 'at greater depth', which means they're above the level expected for their age. Leesa made a deal with him that if he got seven or more greater-depth grades we would give him a Kindle. I didn't say anything, because you have to provide a united front, but I disagreed. 'At greater depth' is out of his control, isn't it? So we're rewarding his ability rather than his effort. You'd like to think we would have rewarded him with a Kindle if all of his grades were 'Needs development' but he was applying himself. But Kindles are expensive so then it's wasted money on a thicko, isn't it?

This is all coming from ideal-parent Romesh, of course. The other day Theo came home and said he'd achieved the highest score in his year for something and I punched the air. So, basically, I'm a huge hypocrite. It does beg the question

'Why?' though. Why am I so happy he achieved the highest score, and why haven't I punched the air on all those occasions he's simply been trying his best? I think it's because we all have it drilled into us that if we achieve at school, we get excellent grades, which means better job prospects, which means more money. And I find that pretty distasteful. I don't like the idea that we equate success with financial gain. What I can support, though, is that better grades and job prospects generally equal better opportunities, which offers my kids something approaching the freedom to choose what they want to do with their lives. If Theo grows up and wants to be a postman I'll be fine with that, so long as I do everything I can to give him the option to become a neuroscientist. And also to convince him that neuroscientists are awesome and being a postman is shit.

What I most want for my children is for them to be happy. And I really have no idea how to prepare them to be the happiest they can be. I guess if they're good people, and do things they believe in, and live to see their eighteenth birthdays, Leesa and I will have done the best we can. And, fingers crossed, Leesa and I are both dead before any psychological issues become apparent.

I'm very happy as a comedian, and I feel this is the best thing I could have done for my life, and for my family. I also believe I wouldn't have become a comedian were it not for the wiring screw-ups that came from my childhood. In other words, had our family not gone through the issues we did, and had I not experienced the trauma that I did, I would not have become a comic. That sort of thing changes you. This is the case for so many people.

Whenever you see musicians or comedians or even entrepreneurs, they always talk of something that happened in their childhood that drove them to wherever they are now. And the same is true for me.

When I was starting out in stand-up, I was invited by Channel 4 to take part in a 'Getting Minorities on TV' event when all the comedians of colour and/or in a wheelchair were gathered together so that some sort of diversity initiative could be met. I'm not against the idea of increased diversity and actively chasing it, but on that occasion I got the feeling that this might have been somebody completing the last task for their yearly appraisal. Jimmy Mulville from Hat Trick, producers of *Have I Got News for You*, was there and I'll never forget what he said: 'If you haven't had something happen to you in your upbringing that has messed you up even a little bit, you should probably leave comedy.'

I'm not saying I've had the toughest life imaginable, but I do think if my parents hadn't had their problems, I would be doing something very different. Going through something like that makes you re-evaluate your relationships with your parents, and what you think about life, which fuels comedy. It's also highly possible that I've just reverse-engineered my upbringing to convince myself I was destined to do stand-up. And that my fuck-ups will somehow help my kids in the long run.

One of the things I struggle with as a parent, and don't believe we think about enough, is what we want for our children. I was inspired to think about this, weirdly, by Crispin Glover, who played George McFly in *Back to the*

Future. If you haven't seen it, I would strongly urge you to watch it as part of the best movie trilogy ever made, alongside *Toy Story* and *Star Wars*. In the film, Marty McFly returns from the past to find he has altered his present and is now living in Paradise. And this is what Crispin Glover had a problem with: the happy ending comprised Marty having a nicer car, the whole family having really good jobs and being super-successful, with his dad now a celebrated author. Crispin's point was that it's a very materialistic way to view happiness. He was immediately removed from the next two movies in a harsh lesson on keeping your opinions to yourself.

That made me think about the default setting we seem to have adopted about educating our children, almost by force, so that they can get what we consider to be good jobs and live what we believe to be happy lives. And I have no idea if this is right. Will my children be happier as lawyers or as starving artists? I have no idea. And I have no idea what I should be doing to ensure they choose the correct path. Which is how I understand why almost all of the parents I know at our kids' school agonize about the performance of their children in tests and assessments.

6.

I Need Love

My teaching days also taught me that if the kids believe you like them and want the best for them, they'll accept any level of bollocking or punishment or classroom control. If they don't, you have absolutely no chance. That has followed me into the stand-up arena, where I often take the piss, as many comedians do, out of someone in the audience. I hope I do it in a way that makes the person feel like we're having a laugh together rather than them being destroyed for the crowd's amusement. Although I do occasionally have to shame hecklers publicly.

I was doing the Big Value show in Edinburgh, (the one that led to me having to stand down as head of sixth form) when I had to step in for one of the acts on the late show. There were two issues that night. One was that I had only twenty minutes of material, and some of the audience from the earlier show, which was mine, had decided to stay to watch the next, which meant they'd see me deliver the same material they'd seen an hour earlier. That meant I'd have to focus on other audience members and try to ignore the burning gazes of the people who knew my punchline about Barack Obama.

The other issue was a drunk woman, who was shouting

during all of the acts. It was relentless. All of the acts had beaten her in heckle combat, which is the point at which most hecklers shut up, but she continued shouting and inter-rupting, ruining one guy's set completely. She was negatively affecting the show, and ordinarily she would have been thrown out, but there were no security staff that night. Then it was my turn to go on, and as soon as I started talking she was shouting. As she interrupted me, I said, 'I'm not a come-dian who's going to put you down. I travel around with a large Asian gang who will meet you outside and slap the shit out of you.' Not great – I was threatening violence. But I was new and desperate. I do want to reiterate that there is no way I would say that now. I would just arrange the beating.

Immediately the woman shut up. I was delighted. Then she got up and walked out with her friends. Result!

The show carried on without incident, and I felt the right-eous heroic admiration of the crowd. As I left, I was greeted by the woman and her friends who were issuing a formal complaint about me to the venue. Darrell Martin, head of Just the Tonic, was hilarious. He said, 'Well, I've spoken to some of the venue staff, and by all accounts you've been a right arsehole, but thanks for your complaint.'

Komedia in Brighton are hot on making sure hecklers get dealt with, but on one occasion it did backfire. I was doing a set about the difficulties in taking your children on holiday when one of the crowd shouted, 'Just sack off the little ragamuffins!'

I was surprised to hear such an old-fashioned word so I said, 'Sorry, mate, did you just use the word "ragamuffin"?'

The Brighton in the crowd came out then as somebody

else said, 'You cannot say that to him. That's racist!' I have no idea how it's racist. It wasn't racist. This person just heard 'ragamuffin', made an association with Jamaican patois and took that to mean the guy was being racist, which I think in itself might be quite racist. Suddenly the bouncers came up and grabbed the guy to throw him out. I started protesting, but they put their hands up to say, 'We've got this, don't worry.' Next thing I knew the guy was being frogmarched out.

I finished my set, then ran outside to find him and get him back into the club, but he had gone. I felt terrible. If by any slim chance he's reading this now, I'd like him to know that I'm sorry. But, really, you shouldn't be so racist, mate.

Teaching, then, had given me some preparation for gigging. Hazelwick, by coincidence, had a vacancy in their maths department around the time I was coming to the end of my training course with them, and they encouraged me to apply for the job, which I did.

My first year as a qualified teacher was difficult, as it is for all new teachers. I remember being given a piece of advice by an old hand. He suggested that, because I was teaching my first lessons with all of these children, I had to show them I wasn't messing about: as soon as a kid stepped out of line for any reason, no matter how trivial, I should absolutely hammer them. After five minutes of vein-popping and shouting, every child in the room would be terrified of me. Then I could behave as I liked because they would always remember that first bollocking and never want to see it again. He didn't mention the fallout from traumatizing the targeted child, but I got the idea. It wasn't in my nature, but I felt it would be arrogant not to try it at least once.

The next day, I saw my year-eight (eleven years old) class and prepared myself to bring the fire. They walked in very quietly, but I could see they were working me out. I put them in their allocated seats and looked for any possible issue that I could leap on. Suddenly a hand was up. 'I've forgotten my pen, sir.'

'Okay. Here's one,' I said weakly, trying to summon some rage. Pathetic. In that moment, I knew I didn't have it in me to bollock kids so I'd have to find a different way to control my classes.

That's not to say I didn't try hard discipline a couple of times. There was a particular kid in my first year of teaching who kept undermining me. I tried all of the techniques I knew to get him onside, but he was impossible. Eventually I took him outside and tried to shout at him. He looked at me like I'd gone insane. Kids cannot be shouted into obedience. It makes absolutely no sense. I never managed to get that kid to cooperate with me but he taught me a lesson: I needn't think I had all the answers.

At the end of my first year, a vacancy came up for an assistant head of sixth form and I decided it was something I'd like to do. I applied for the job and got it. This was really exciting: it meant I was involved in the care of the students, not just teaching. I felt it could be really rewarding.

It quickly became apparent that I should not have got the job. It was given to me because the school believed I was good with students and had strong interpersonal skills, which would be good for dealing with parents. Not only had they massively overestimated my abilities on that front, but the job also required serious organizational skills and the ability to deal with scheduling. And I couldn't do that at all. I was monumentally bad at it. I would turn up to assemblies wondering why the person delivering it wasn't there, only to be reminded that I was supposed to have arranged for someone to speak. I would have no idea what was coming up on the academic calendar and my eye for detail seemed to be the lazy one.

Every year, the lower sixth (year twelve) were taken to Exeter University to have a series of talks and activities to prepare them for, or give them an idea of, higher education. For some reason I ended up as the organizer, even though I was worse than the students at being on top of things. The idea was to set up so many things during the day that the students would be too knackered at the end of it to sneak out of their accommodation for bevvies or sex. Also, we would visit every student's room at the end of the evening and check they were in there ready to sleep. As there were 150-odd students, we staff would divvy up this responsibility between us.

One night, we were just finishing our 'Goodnight, please don't shag each other,' patrol, when a teacher returned to tell us that one of his students was missing. Now this was worrying as everybody else had come back and reported that everyone was present and correct. Which meant that one lad was missing on his own. I ran to the boy's room and let myself in with the master key. Sure enough he wasn't there, and members of staff who were inclined to go a bit OTT were saying things like 'Don't touch anything. This is a crime scene.'

We started to search the site for him. After about five minutes I received a phone call. 'We've found him.' It turned out that one of the staff hadn't checked his area properly and a few of the boys had made a break for the student bar.

I arrived at his room to find the boy ashen-faced and my boss in full-flow bollocking. The others had apparently been led by this lad and had been given grade-two bollockings, but he was getting the full hairdryer. My boss was shouting about how he had let down the school, his parents, himself . . . It was all very standard except that the boy, apart from looking sorry for himself, kept farting loudly every thirty seconds or so. It was so unbelievable that I was pretty convinced I was imagining it. What confused things further was that the lad kept apologizing, but I couldn't figure out whether it was for what he had done or for the farts. My uncertainty was settled when my boss said, 'Now go to bed or the toilet, or whatever the hell you have to do!'

Miraculously, the following year I ended up as senior head of sixth form and had a team of two people. The common room seemed to have become an ongoing issue: every night I would be in my office and one of the caretakers would appear and say, 'Could I show you this, please?' And I would have to follow him in and shake my head at the crisps on the floor and bits of bread that had been thrown about, and assure him I would do something about it. The next day I would tell the sixth form in assembly that if this carried on I would close the common room. I would be in my office that evening and one of the caretakers would come in and say, 'Could I show you this, please?' You get the idea.

I imagine you're wondering why I didn't close the common room. I did once and it was a bloody nightmare. Two hundred kids were displaced into other areas of the school. It was like the end of days. So I just had to keep shaking my head with the caretaker and not tell him that this would probably happen every day.

What made the whole experience weirder for me was that *I* had been responsible for that common room being closed when I was a student at Hazelwick. Me and another lad were just getting into cigarettes and weed in sixth form and nipped into the common-room toilets for a quick fag. We were trying to wash our hands afterwards to avoid detection when we started pissing about with the tap and trying to get each other wet. All of a sudden the tap broke and water was shooting out of the top. We ran.

About an hour later we returned to find the common-room foyer flooded. Members of staff were interrogating students about what had happened, threatening to close the common room if nobody owned up. We agreed to keep schtum and the common room was closed for about two weeks.

Now, I agree, that was a proper dick move, but in my defence I was seventeen and everyone is a dick at that age, right? I honestly don't think I'd always been one. I was in a weird place after what had happened to my family so I was being a fake rebel or something. This meant I would walk around the school thinking I was a proper hoodlum, staring people out and bunking lessons. It was the student equivalent of a mid-life crisis.

Now that I was living on a council estate I was getting

to know some of the kids round there and pretending to be hard. There was one other Asian guy who lived nearby and I think he was playing the same game as me but happened to know a few people in the area. He told me he had a crew, and if I had any problems at Hazelwick, he'd deal with them. I sort of believed him but also thought he was full of shit.

The next day I was walking down to Tesco for lunch when I spotted a commotion in the car park. There were loads of cars in a group and people gathered round. I was intrigued. It didn't even occur to me that it might be about me. As I approached the crowd, I saw what looked like every Asian kid in Sussex gathered in a huge group. They were led by my new friend, who had taken great pains to tell anyone who cared to listen that they were with me and would smash up anyone who gave me any problems.

Jesus Christ. I was mortified. I'd had no idea this would happen. It was one of the most pathetic things I'd ever seen and it was being done in my name. I'd spent my school life wishing I had a gang and now one had turned up, made up almost exclusively of people I didn't know.

As soon as I got back to school I was hauled into the head of sixth form's office and asked for a list of names of the 'gang' I was running. Word had obviously got through that either some sort of gang warfare was going on or Tesco had opened an immigration centre. Whichever, I was to blame. I was told there was no place at Hazelwick for gangs and that if I didn't hand over names I would be asked to leave the sixth form. This was a sticky little pickle. On the one hand I risked ending my education and,

when my mum found out, my life, or I could end up protesting my innocence, shopping somebody who clearly
had gang connections and knew my home address. I
was partly tempted to just hand over a series of generic
Asian names and let her get on with thinking they were all
called Raj Patel.

It was a nightmare, and I deserved it. I'd spent the previous few months walking around like I was some sort of
gangster and now it had come to bite me on the arse.

Fortunately, as is the way with most school investiga-
tions, it sort of petered out. I was very lucky. I say that, but
I didn't put my second opportunity to good use. I slacked
and bunked and did no work and got a set of A-level grades
worthy of a wannabe gangster. My surname had more As
than me. And Ns. And Gs. This really doesn't work.

What I loved about running the sixth form was also what
made it so challenging and stressful: you never knew what
was going to happen, and a lot of scenarios were without
precedent so you had to figure out the best course of action
based on instinct.

Because school isn't compulsory beyond the age of sixteen, there was a much less official process of disciplining
students. Usually, you would warn the student first. Then,
if things didn't improve, you would send a letter home
warning the parents. Finally, as a last resort, you would
exclude that student. This was normally because they were
not attending lessons or causing issues when they did. If
they'd had those systems when I was a teenager I would
definitely have been excluded.

One student, of Pakistani origin, was being extremely

disruptive in lessons. I always found it strange that sixth-formers would disrupt class because they had chosen to come back voluntarily, but many stayed on because they had no idea what else to do. They behaved as if they were being held against their will. This kid was acting up to teachers and generally being a dick. I called him in and warned him about his behaviour. He was suitably remorseful. Days later I received more complaints that he was being a nightmare. I called him back in and informed him I would be sending a letter to his parents. He went back into lessons and was still misbehaving so I sent yet another letter. Still no change. Eventually I decided to call his mum in to explain that I would be asking her son to leave. She didn't speak any English and came with a friend who acted as her interpreter.

It transpired that this kid was a genius. Because his mum didn't speak English, he was 'translating' the letters home and telling her he had been commended for excellent achievements. That was the impression the interpreter was under too. When I explained the truth, the interpreter looked shocked, turned to the mum and said something in Urdu. The mum burst into tears, rocking back and forth and wailing. The interpreter explained that the boy's family just wanted him to do well: couldn't I give him another chance? Of course she was very upset, and had only just found out that her son wasn't a high achiever, that he was super-disruptive and had been lying to her. I still felt the correct decision was to exclude him, which meant another forty-five minutes of her rocking back and forth in the office. I almost tried to reassure her that he had displayed a level of ingenuity that suggested he was probably going to do very well in life. He was actually a ledge.

We also had a girl who was, for want of a better term, a bit of a princess. She was extremely confident and entitled, just the sort of person I usually hate. I didn't quite hate her but she was certainly difficult. She had been going out with one of the alpha lads and they had suddenly split up. He had started seeing another girl. She was very upset about this and decided that having to watch them walking around openly constituted bullying: she wanted me to do something about it.

She came into my office, sat down without being asked, and started telling me how I obviously didn't care about bullying because I was allowing her to be bullied by that pair. She wanted me to ask him to leave the school, or she would be taking further action, she threatened. It was all very Single White Female. When I said I'd look into it, but that it was unlikely to be classed as bullying, she flipped out, telling me I didn't care about her. She went to storm out of the office, but couldn't get the door open. I spent the next thirty seconds watching her try to open a door. I could have told her to push the handle the other way, but I really felt the door was teaching her a valuable lesson that things don't always work exactly the way you want them to.

One of the most challenging moments in my head of sixth form career became known to the sixth-form team as 'Fort Gate'. One evening I was again summoned to the common room so I could shake my head and look appalled, when the caretaker drew my attention to a new structure at one end of the room. It was a fort. A fort that had been assembled from the furniture. It was a proper structure with little gaps in it, like arrow slits, I assume to throw food from. The caretaker said, 'I think this shows you that it has got out of control in here.' Which was true. But also, they'd built a bloody fort. That's cool as shit, isn't it? I couldn't help feeling a little bit proud.

That presented a problem. The head teacher had got wind of the situation and wanted it dealt with strongly. He wanted the culprits banned from the common room in no uncertain terms. The next morning we asked for those responsible to come forward, and the guilty parties appeared. Already I was impressed because, as you know, I wouldn't have owned up. I asked them to wait outside the office and then spoke to the two assistant heads of sixth. I explained to them that we had to issue an almighty bollocking to these students, but there was no way that anyone could use the word 'fort' because it would make me laugh. The whole thing was utterly ridiculous but we had to keep up appearances, which meant not cracking up during the reckoning.

We got them in and took turns to explain how disappointed we were, when we were actually impressed. We used words like 'structure' and 'thing' and managed to get through it. But I wondered if the kids thought it was ridiculous too. I've since spoken to them and they told me they thought it was. Yes, they were wrong for wasting their time like that, and they should have put everything away afterwards but, in their defence, they made a fort! That's precisely what kids should be doing.

When I was teaching at Hazelwick I went on a trip to Ghana with the sixth form. Hazelwick sponsored a village primary-school teacher there and each year around seven sixth-formers went to see the work that was being done and then spend some time at another school in the capital to counteract the belief that all Africans were starving.

Leesa was on that trip. I hadn't spoken to her much, mainly because she was a drama teacher and I was prejudiced against those barefoot 'call me by my first name' freaks. However, as the trip went on we began talking and really got on. I was already in a relationship, and certainly not looking to fall in love, but I really did connect with Leesa in a way I hadn't done with anyone before. I've read enough memoirs to know that people always describe their partner as the most wonderful, funny, intelligent person ever, and I always think it's because they suspect their other half is going to read it. So, Leesa, if you read this, I was mainly looking at your arse.

One night just before the end of the trip, when the kids had gone to bed, Leesa, Lianne (the trip leader) and I sat and talked over a beer. Lianne went to bed, leaving Leesa and me to carry on talking. We were still talking when the kids started emerging from their rooms again. I became concerned for two reasons: I had been up all night talking to another woman, and I was now going to be supervising a school trip without having slept. But I was mainly worried about the other-woman thing. I was in a relationship.

Nothing had happened between Leesa and me, and the rest of the trip passed without incident, but something had changed and I suppose I knew it.

I felt sad saying goodbye to Leesa, but only in the way you get a bit of post-holiday blues. At work our paths rarely crossed. A few weeks later, though, I was at home doing the vacuuming when I saw a photo I'd been given from the trip of the kids and staff, Leesa included. I looked at it and realized how much I missed her. It felt like an ache and a sadness that we weren't in Ghana having that chat all over again. And I realized I had strong feelings for her. I also realized that, even if nothing ever happened with Leesa, I had to end my relationship because people don't have feelings like that unless there's a major problem.

Leesa and I soon moved in together. My parents and brother could not have been more supportive, my friends too, despite initial scepticism because things had moved so quickly.

Leesa and I made a real effort to keep our relationship away from school and certainly the students. I didn't fancy having loads of students asking me if I was 'giving Miss Maynard one'. I'm a firm believer in honesty and would have felt compelled to tell them I was giving her several and was getting rather good at it. Mind you, she is a trained actor.

Our relationship got validation that I never expected. A few months after Leesa and I moved in together, we were all at a wedding, getting pretty hammered, and my dad grabbed Leesa by the arm and said, 'I just wanted to say thank you for giving us our son back.' I don't know if he was under the impression that she had secured my release from Ghana but it was very special. Dad's obviously no longer with us, but my one hope is that my mum will be as understanding when I bin Leesa off for someone more glamorous now I've been on TV a bit.

In truth I could never do that. Leesa has been through so much in this relationship. When we were struggling, I was very conscious of the fact I was dragging the family through some very difficult times so that I could 'chase a dream'. And not a particularly noble one. Although I wanted to make it as a comedian, if she had ever turned to me and said, 'You need to give this up now', I would have done so in a heartbeat. But she never did. And when I asked her down the line if she ever would have, she said she never had any doubt that I would make a decent career of it. Which sounds like the sort of thing you'd say after everything has worked out. Nevertheless, she has been through some bloody tough times with me, so I owe it to her never to be disloyal – unless the other person is incredibly hot. Of course, if Leesa happens to have dropped me by the time you read this, let me take this opportunity to say that I knew all along that she was a heartless bitch.

While Leesa was turning my world on its head, I was getting into another significant relationship with one of the other guys in the sixth-form team, Mark Lotsu. He was charismatic and charming, and became a very good friend, long before the days of giving up his time to drive me to gig after gig. He was an exceptional teacher, and the students had an admiration and love for him that most teachers could only dream of. He was a top bloke.

When I left teaching to pursue comedy full time, we drifted apart. Mark went to teach at a boarding school, and I just became incredibly busy. We spoke every now and again, but it was increasingly infrequent. A few years later Mark was going through a stressful period in his life and we would speak a lot more, as I tried to support him through it, as he had supported me at the beginning of my comedy career. Then we got busy again and stopped talking.

About six months ago, as I write, we met up for dinner. Mark told me about his new girlfriend and that he had just moved to Leicester. He was working a number of jobs, but seemed to be in high spirits. We had a nice evening and, as we left, talked about how we should have a drink soon. That was the last time I saw him.

I was filming a show called *The Misadventures of Romesh Ranganathan*, in which I travelled to countries that people tend not to go to: I wanted to see if they were actually worth visiting. One of these was Ethiopia, and one night we stayed outdoors at a village on the Eritrean border so were basically off the grid for about thirty-six hours. We were unable to speak to or text anybody.

We moved on to a hotel, which was to be our base for the next couple of days. As I connected to the wi-fi, my phone started going crazy. Loads of messages were flooding through, all saying things like 'Sorry about Mark' and 'Can you believe what's happened to Mark?' Weirdly, because I'd always thought of Mark as invincible, it took me a minute or so to register that the messages were about him. But when I thought they might be, I phoned his best friend. He explained that it was unclear what had happened, but it looked as if Mark had killed himself.

I was devastated. I couldn't believe he would have done it, not with so many friends and loved ones around him, and a life that seemed so full of positives. Everything had seemed so great. Clearly that is not how depression works, and I knew that, but it didn't stop me asking myself questions. I was distraught, and went to my room to process the news. I'm still processing it, and still upset now. And the question that I have not stopped asking myself is 'Could I have done more to help Mark?'

I needed to do something to counter the feeling that I had somehow let him down, so I asked about becoming an ambassador for CALM, a charity involved in helping men deal with their feelings and connect with each other in a bid to reduce male suicide. I don't think this role will ever enable me to feel okay about what happened with Mark, but I've come to accept that. I realize this is a pretty depressing end to the chapter, but the beginning of the next chapter is super-upbeat, I promise.

7.

Lose Yourself

The death of my father led to a pretty dark period in my life.* My brother and I immediately became concerned about Mum's wellbeing. She was living in a house that was mortgaged to the eyeballs and also now had to deal with sorting out Dad's finances.

After Dad had come out of prison, he had gradually worked his way back up to where he was before, culminating in him being appointed financial director of a book export company in north London. He really enjoyed his time there, particularly as the owners were huge Arsenal fans.

I don't know whether I'm an Arsenal fan because of Dad or if he was an Arsenal fan because of me. I had always assumed that because he first lived in north London when he arrived from Sri Lanka he had adopted the Gunners and passed it on to the family, but he claimed it was my enthusiasm that made him a big fan.

It wasn't until I started going that he ever went to see them play live. The first time we went, he behaved as if he'd literally just arrived in the country. He bought every piece

* I lied when I said the start of the chapter would be upbeat.

of dodgy merch from the surrounding stalls. He looked a lot like an older Prince Akeem from *Coming to America* when he arrives in New York from Zamunda and tries to blend in. On the way to the ground, Dad decided he wanted fried chicken urgently so we detoured to get him some, with both of us knowing this would make us late (Ranganathans don't do punctuality) and I sat agitated as he ate. Little did I know this was only the beginning. We made it to the game and watched Arsenal triumph over Chelsea 3–1. It was amazing. So amazing, in fact, that my dad became convinced that the fried chicken detour had affected the result, and from then on insisted he had fried chicken every time he went to a match. Did I mention how inevitable his heart attack was?

Perhaps as a result of those chicken-fuelled days out, I have the same risk of heart disease as a sumo wrestler, and am currently spending a lot of time trying to avoid my wheezy demise by going to spin classes and personal training. I have very low willpower, though, so in all likelihood as you're reading this I'll have given it all up and will be eating a pizza. Or I'll be dead.

Pizzas have been ruined by my veganism. This is because the key ingredient of pizza is cheese. Cheese serves so many purposes on a pizza. I remember as a kid thinking it looked so incredible when they pulled up a slice of pizza and the melty cheese formed strings of delicious chewy dairyness across the plate. Of course, now I know that cheese is morally reprehensible.

I also now know that pizza is a scam. The melted cheese conceals the fact it is hugely overpriced. Since going vegan I have ordered pizza without cheese many times, because vegan cheese hasn't reached pizza places yet in the UK, and also because vegan cheese is fucking unacceptable. When I first became a vegan, I knew that cheese was going to be the biggest issue. Science backs me up on this because research has shown that cheese is as addictive as hard drugs. My first priority as a vegan, therefore, was to source a great vegan cheese. In my first year, I reckon I spent about six hundred pounds on the stuff: Sheese, Cheeze, Chease. It's all shite. Plus you can't get a vegan cheese that multitasks. You know how when you get a block of Cheddar, you can either grate it onto salads, eat it in slices, or melt it into a toastie? Vegan cheese can't do that. It's the male equivalent of cheese: it can only do one thing. So you have to buy one for eating in slices, one for grating onto salads, and one for melting. And it all tastes like shit.

Whenever I've said this onstage, a vegan cheese company has got in touch and said, 'Saw you're not convinced by vegan cheese. I think you should try this,' then sent me a box of turd. I'm happy to be convinced otherwise, but I can't see it happening anytime soon.

The problem with ordering a pizza without cheese is the pizza ruse is exposed. Melted cheese not only makes everything taste incredible but also sticks all of the other ingredients to the base. When you order a vegan pizza you hand over about fifteen quid and receive a box containing a flatbread with some vegetables in the corner. And a pot of very un-vegan garlic butter. Who is not yet convinced by the heart-attack-inducing qualities of a pizza that they also feel the need to dip the thing in butter? I can only assume it's meant to be a pleasurable form of suicide.

All this pizza eating led me to the gym, which I find absolutely torturous. Apparently when you first start going you experience the buzz of working out, then hit a wall where it feels horrible. Once you get past that, you start to enjoy and even crave it. I only have the wall. Regardless of how often I've been going, whether I've started back after a while, or have been going for a few months, all I feel is wall. It's like I'm repeatedly smashing my dick into a wall, then clapping two bricks against it until it's completely severed from my body. And then jumping up and down on it wearing shoes made of bricks. What I'm saying is: I don't enjoy the gym.

One of my biggest problems with the gym is what it does to people. I don't mean physically – lots of my friends go to the gym and look amazing. They achieve incredible things, like looking forward to summer holidays, being able to wear a T-shirt without crying, or seeing photos of themselves without entering two months of depression. I've lost count of the number of photos I've seen of myself where one of my buttons looks like it's screaming in agony under the pressure of having to keep my shirt together. My wife and I have sometimes used these pictures as a form of contraception.

My problem is what it does to people mentally. People who regularly visit gyms become these positively aspirational, goal-visualizing, progress-updating bell-ends. Apparently it's impossible to visit the gym without posting something on Facebook, like: 'Pushed it to the max this morning, feeling great and achieving great, now to tackle the rest of the day #wellness #pushtheenvelope #goalsmasher #lifeiswhatyoumakeit.' Everybody who goes to the gym is so obsessed with goals that they seem unaware of how pointless those goals are. You're just trying to look great. That's not a noble ambition. It's trivial. Which is fine. But let's not pretend that it's some incredible selfless calling. You just want to look nice on the beach in Portugal. I'd just like to wear a T-shirt without wanting to cry.

I've given up trying to look nice. I've been liberated from that by forty years of hideous physique and the lazy eye that makes face-to-face conversation with me off-putting. My main aim is to stay alive. To my family's history of heart disease I can also add a belly and moobs, which I'm frequently reminded by *Men's Health* are the main give-away signs that my system should have shut down when I was thirty. So, my main motivation is for my kids to still have me around when they hit their teens. But you can't post, 'Another workout to delay my death today. Hoping I don't have a heart attack before 40 #heartdisease #history-ofitinthefamily #pleasecanInotdie.'

A few years ago I was asked to a do a gig to support the British Heart Foundation. David Blood, whom I'd met on the Brighton circuit, had narrowly avoided death by heart attack and had resolved to help with the cause. He had set up an annual gig, with all proceeds going to the charity. He asked me if I would be willing to take part and I agreed, thinking it was a positive thing to do to offset the negative karma I regularly accrue from being a bit of a prick.

The night before the gig, I was doing *Mock the Week*. The recording had gone fine and I was in the pub across the road from the studios having a post-match pint. I had a look at Twitter. What I found was a series of tweets from various vegan activists telling me I was an arsehole for agreeing to take part in the gig as the British Heart Foundation test on animals. The tweets said I should be ashamed and were demanding my immediate withdrawal from the gig. I looked at my Facebook page to find numerous posts from people calling me a 'fucking bastard', accompanied by numerous photos of dogs having been slaughtered in the name of research. I was also bombarded with private messages telling me I'd lost the support of the vegan community and had let down many people: there would be a concerted effort to boycott me.

I don't know how I feel about all of this. I wasn't aware of the animal testing, which I was told made me an ignorant prick rather than just a prick. I was in shock, though, at how all of this had stemmed from me just agreeing to do a gig for a mate who had been through a lot. And as I had lost my father to a sudden heart attack, the issue resonated with me. I did think about pulling the gig. I even contacted my agent, who said that they would support any decision I made, but also reminded me that social networks are a haven for twats. I decided to go ahead with it: I didn't want to let Dave down, and I didn't know what my position was on the whole thing. I certainly wasn't going to take major action based on the subjective accounts of some nutcase on Twitter.

The gig was at Brighton Komedia, and I turned up at the venue to see a protest against the gig and my involvement. Thankfully, they didn't see me: I spotted what was going on from a distance and used the back entrance. When I arrived, Dave told me that some of the protesters had demanded to know why I was involved. I have a number of problems with this – but the main one is the assumption that I have to acquiesce to their viewpoint. I'm totally open to discussion or debate, but the militant forcing of views is completely counterproductive. The way I was treated was akin to them believing that in my act that night I intended to spend my twenty minutes onstage slaughtering dogs and laughing about it. Which would certainly have been no stranger than many of the acts I'd seen on the open-mic circuit. What it did achieve, though, was to make me reluctant to get involved in the promotion of vegan causes. I don't want to be associated with that militant bullshit. Not until they make a decent cheese.

Now, spin classes are weird. They feel a bit like joining a cult. I go on my own mostly but sometimes with my wife, who struggles to contain her laughter at my lack of coordination. An instructor puts on some loud music of their choice, then starts screaming at you as you pretend to increase the resistance on your bike. I find this a great way to exercise as my inherent laziness means I won't do anything unless someone's shouting at me or there are serious consequences to giving up. If I really wanted a six-pack the only way to achieve it would be to arrange for someone to have my family held at gunpoint, and even then the chances would only be slightly higher than 50 per cent.

It was for this reason that I opted to have some personal training sessions. I use a friend from school for this, but he's well versed in the 'push it to the envelope max' school of working out. High-intensity training seems to be the accepted way forward now, and this has been widely heralded as great news. I, however, am not convinced. The idea is that you pack a more intense workout into a shorter time, achieve results and get on with whatever your day entails. But it makes each and every workout absolutely horrendous. My personal trainer will take me to a regular piece of equipment that I've seen and used many times before, then tell me that if I want to 'maximize gains' I need to lasso it with a gym rope, tie it to my waist and drag it round the gym while doing the Macarena. He then tells me it's normal to bleed from the eyes and that shitting out of my bladder means it's really working. He also has the slightly irritating habit of trying to engage me in conversation as I'm in the middle of dying, and he likes to wait until one of my arms falls off before saying, 'Let's see if you can push out two more reps.' Having said all of this, he's a very nice man, who deals with my lack of coordination and muscle atrophy with extreme patience. I do sometimes wonder if he's pushing me so hard because he wants results or because he's looking for a bit of a laugh.

But I was talking about my dad. He eventually bought out the book export company and moved it to East Grinstead so he didn't have to commute too far from Crawley. He spent his lunch breaks at a pub down the road called the Prince of Wales. It was a sticky-carpeted dog-on-a-string type of place, and he fell in love with it. So much so that he sold the company and bought the pub, much to Mum's utter dismay. Dad was a proper pisshead, and we were all worried about him drinking too much, so I remember having a chat with him about what he might do if people offered to buy him drinks to excess. He would always find a way to politely decline, he said. Less than six months later I was watching him in the pub, absolutely battered, singing along to Bob Marley's 'Jamming' using only the words 'We're jamming' throughout the whole piece – verse and chorus – then demanding a song he knew better, requesting Punjabi MC and singing, 'We're jamming,' through that too.

Dad turned the pub into an Arsenal fan's dream. He would show all of the Arsenal games and spend the entirety of the matches screaming his tits off at the television. On one occasion, we were beaten by Manchester United at home 4–2. The pub was rammed and people were going mad. Dad had had enough. The game finished, he walked up to the screen, switched off the telly, and shouted, 'Everybody, fuck off!'

He also helped me get stand-up experience. I had been moaning that I wasn't getting enough stage time, so he suggested I put on a regular gig at the pub and host it. I had about seven minutes of material at the time, and no idea how to host, so it felt like exactly the kind of challenge I should be taking on. I started up a monthly night called The Last Stand-up. The regulars were furious and made it clear that if any of the acts were shit they would let them know. But then they also said things like 'We were worried about an Asian landlord but your dad is one of the good ones.'

My brother, Dinesh, and I also did a bit of DJing for Dad as he was being messed about by his regular guy. He gave us the money to buy equipment and then we became his regular entertainment, which essentially meant playing CD decks while people ignored us and complained about women and immigrants. We must have been doing something right as we started getting offered outside work.

We didn't have any aspirations to become DJs so we'd do a gig, then head to a bar and spend exactly what we'd made on the same night. Once we were playing for an older crowd at East Grinstead Working Men's Club. These were always the most annoying gigs as people would come up and make dreadful requests, then stand in front of you with their arms folded until you played Dexys Midnight Runners again. Everyone was battered.

One man was dancing like his wife had just left him and dancing was all he had left. He was dancing so badly we nearly turned the music off to save any further embarrassment to anyone who might know him. He was dancing so badly that he stumbled head first into one of our speakers. It was a rollercoaster of emotions. On one hand, he might have hurt himself, and on the other, what the hell had he done to our speakers? He got up almost immediately and staggered off, with a couple of people looking after him. My brother and I had barely finished processing the events when an ambulance turned up and the man was wheeled out by paramedics. Insane. Even odder, other people were continuing to dance as all of this was going on, presumably in a desperate attempt to keep the party going.

We were faced with the unusual social-etiquette question of how long after the arrival of paramedics you should wait before turning the volume back up. We gave it about five minutes, until East Grinstead's working men were starting to look annoyed, then dropped some more beats to stave off a riot.

My dad's death revealed that his financial situation was a house of cards. He had spent the last few years of his life trying to compensate my mum for the way he had treated her previously. He had bought her a lovely car and a huge house, but had taken on a lot of debt to finance them. He had also hidden the fact that the pub was haemorrhaging money. My dad died in December. Dinesh became convinced that we needed to keep the pub going to capture the earnings from the Christmas period so we reopened it between us, with nothing approaching a clue about how to be landlords.

I was in a bit of a bind as I had just left teaching and had no regular wage coming in. With a young family, I was seriously concerned about how we were going to survive, as well as help my mum out. I wondered if we'd be able to manage. As it turns out we wouldn't. Dinesh resented me for not spending enough time helping him with everything, and we started to argue a lot. I don't know if this was just part of the grieving process but it's fair to say it affected our relationship badly. My brother has sometimes suggested that I'm not focused enough on family, and this seemed to be further evidence of my lack of commitment.

My brother is essentially a better version of me. He is younger, slimmer, funnier, more handsome and kinder. And I am guilty of letting him down a bit. Dinesh expects a lot and delivers a lot, and I am the exact opposite. For that reason, we often clash, but despite that, we're very close. This period following Dad's death really did jeopardize that, but we've made things up now.

As well as falling out with my brother and failing to support my mum adequately, Leesa and I were struggling to pay bills, the house looked a bit like a squat, and we could only afford the bare minimum of groceries to keep us alive. In hindsight, starting a comedy career just as we'd had kids was probably not the wisest move, but you're reading a book by the prick who did that so it's worked out. Unless this book is released posthumously.

I had the biggest difficulty with the fact that I had caused all this by being incredibly self-indulgent. I still find the idea that I should be paid to stand onstage and chat shit a little bit embarrassing. I would have found it easier to deal with had I been striving to end obesity or travelling back in time to kill Katie Hopkins before she said anything.

There are a number of incidences of being broke that stick out in the mind. Christmas is a particularly lucrative time for comedians, although the gigs are the worst. If you've been to a comedy night around Christmas you'll know. The office party planner decides it would be good to go to comedy this year, and then twenty-five people, one of whom once watched Lee Evans, go to a club to eat, drink and sit in silence in front of a comedian whose dad recently died and is struggling to make ends meet. Worse, you will often get the 'office joker/bell-end' who finds it unbelievable that anyone is as funny as him/her (it's him) and heckles, screams or gets his dick out. I have had so many shit Christmas gigs.

I did Up the Creek about a week after Dad died. That sounds insane, but I really thought it would be good for me to get straight back into things, plus I really needed the money. Up the Creek is a great comedy club and I love playing there, but the audiences can be feisty, to say the least. I started my set, feeling proud of myself for getting up onstage and doing twenty minutes of stand-up, like a brave little soldier, when a bloke in the front row decided to give me a racist heckle. That heckle was one of the most effective I've ever faced. It was so effective that I'm actually slightly nervous to divulge it here. What the bloke did was deliver a 'bud bud ding ding' to me. There was a lot to admire in the way he did it. First, he said, 'Bud bud ding ding' – that's proper old school and I respect that. Second, he said it only loud enough for me and his mates to hear, which meant that if I addressed it, I'd be drawing attention to it to people who weren't aware it had happened. Third, and possibly the most impressive of this heckle's attributes, he repeated it every minute or so during my set. I performed the whole lot without acknowledging I was having 'bud bud ding ding' repeated at me from the front row. If that bloke reads this, which is unlikely, well played. You're a prick.

Another festive gig that sticks in the mind was in Tunbridge Wells. The crowd were being served Christmas dinner before the compère introduced the opening act: me. I went on and performed for twenty minutes to complete silence. Jeff Innocent, a comedian who was a particular favourite of Dad's, walked in and through the room to get backstage. During the break I went over to say hello to him, hoping he either hadn't noticed I was dying or wouldn't mention it. He gestured outside: 'Can you hear that, Rom? They're making more noise during the break than they did in your fucking act!' It was a long drive home. I should probably mention that Jeff is a mate and it was a great slam, but it got me right in the balls.

One Christmas I was doing a weekend for Just the Tonic, the chain of comedy clubs run by Darrell Martin, who you've already met. I will always have a soft spot for Darrell as he was one of the first promoters ever to book me for weekends, and he agreed I could do his prestigious Big Value Edinburgh show, the one that led to me being reprimanded at school.

We did have an altercation, though. In 2013 I was planning on doing my first solo show in Edinburgh where Darrell ran an amazing venue called the Tron. I had seen loads of acts like Nick Helm and Eddie Pepitone deliver amazing gigs there so I was keen to perform there too. Darrell told me that if I wanted it I could have the space. Great news. I was signed to Lisa Thomas Management at the time and told them that Darrell had promised me the venue. They said they didn't want me to take it. They had already lined up another venue and were committed. They explained I had to tell him I wasn't doing it.

I did what I usually do in these situations: I went into hiding. Had I told Darrell straight away, he would have been miffed but would have got over it, but I'm pretty spineless when it comes to confrontation. Instead of dealing with things head on, my chosen strategy is to let them drag on until I'm forced to tackle the situation and guaranteed to upset everyone involved. I've become famous for it with my wife and agent and they now militate against it after years of trying to change my habits. I completely agree with you, by the way, that it's a bit pathetic to recognize a flaw and do nothing to tackle it. Let's not talk about it.

So I didn't tell Darrell. For ages. And then one day about a month later I was sitting waiting to start one of his gigs when it occurred to me that I had to tell him. Just before I went on I emailed him to say that, sadly, I would not be able to take his venue. I closed my laptop and ran onstage to do my set.

Little did I know that as I was delivering it the cyber shit was hitting the fan. Darrell was furious. I came offstage to see a vitriolic email, and informing me that all of my gigs with him were pulled with immediate effect. He also took the lovely step of copying in my agent. Now not only did they know I had taken ages to tell him, they also knew that I had lost work as a result of my inactivity/spinelessness/being a twat. It was horrible. Darrell really let loose. In fairness to him, he contacted me a couple of days later to apologize for losing his temper and offering me the work back.

He has given me so much work over the years, and was the first person to give me the prestigious New Year's Eve spot at his club in Nottingham. These gigs, surprisingly, are lovely. This is mainly because they take place earlier when people aren't too battered, and the crowds seem to be in a much better mood than they are just before Christmas. I decided it might be nice to perform in a suit for New Year's Eve, even though I have the figure of a man who, in a suit, looks like he's just conned a pensioner out of a double-glazing deposit.

Nevertheless, I did the gig and had such a great time that I got completely and utterly battered. I saw in the New Year with Nottingham strangers, then stumbled to my

Premier Inn to soak up the first day of January. On entering my room I attempted to get undressed but found it
incredibly difficult to remove one of my shoes. Impossible,
in fact. I was in such a good mood, though, that I decided
not to let it kill the buzz and took off everything else. And
by everything I mean everything. I ended up completely
naked apart from my right shoe. And then I started to get
worried because every time I tried to undo my lace, it got
tighter. In my drunken state, I convinced myself that if
this carried on I'd give myself some circulatory issue and
might lose my foot.

I started to think about my options. I know this might
not seem like the high-stakes drama you read about in
some memoirs, but I was really starting to panic. I was
naked with one shoe on. I actually spent a few minutes
contemplating asking Reception if they could send a
member of staff to help me, but I figured that was above
and beyond the call of duty, as well as being a horrendous way for a member of the Premier Inn staff to start
the New Year: trying to de-shoe a fat, sobbing, naked
Asian man.

Eventually I decided to cut myself out of the shoe.
Which sounds easy. Except that in a Premier Inn hotel
room there are no knives. I don't know if this is a policy,
but what I do now know is that you cannot cut a shoelace
with a teaspoon. After a few minutes it occurred to me
that my most useful tool would be my house keys. And
there I was at three a.m., butt naked and sawing through
my shoe with a key. When I broke free of it, I was euphoric.
I had solved a problem. I had been a prisoner and, through

my own ingenuity, I had freed myself. I felt like I'd survived a *Saw* movie. And now I had only one shoe to wear as I walked to the train station.

My darkest time, though, was one Christmas when I'd arrived in Nottingham to do the Friday and Saturday nights with what I thought was twenty pounds in my bank account, which would enable me to eat over the weekend. On arrival, when I checked my bank balance, a debit had gone through for twenty-one pounds and I now had nothing. Bleak. I was going to have to ration the hotel bourbon biscuits and wait it out till I got to the club and they offered me food. I honestly believe that these are the periods when you reflect the most. I hadn't been eating properly for a while because we were skint, and I remember sitting alone in the hotel after the first gig, broke and hungry and just thinking, How the fuck am I still so fat?

I finally realized that I had driven the family into a cul-de-sac when I couldn't afford to pay the road tax on our car. I told Leesa I had some money due from a gig and that if we could manage for a couple of weeks I'd pay it as soon as the money came in. A week or so later we came home and the car was gone. I immediately phoned the police. They informed me that the car had been impounded as it wasn't taxed and I would have to pay to have it returned. I asked how much that would be and they told me it would cost £150 a day on top of £300 to get it back. I thanked them, put the phone down and told Leesa we no longer had a car. She did not complain but I could see she was distraught. I had just made her life a lot more difficult and all for what felt like a vanity project. And that is why I'd do anything in the world to repay her for going through all of that with me. I'm not bringing a lot to the table on my best day so for her to stick with me as I took us to the bread line is something I'll never forget. Even when I get the opportunity to leave her for a hotter celeb wife, I'll make sure I keep in touch.

It was experiences like this that led me to become frustrated with comedy. I also felt that Lisa Thomas Management were not particularly helpful in guiding me through the difficult period after Dad had passed away. And I had started to suspect they didn't know what to do with me. Most of their other acts were young, shiny presenter types and I was more of an 'ugly' comedian. I felt they weren't putting me forward for much and I began to realize that they might not have a lot of faith in me.

Just before my first Edinburgh show, I was approached by Flo at Off the Kerb. Off the Kerb were and are one of the biggest comedy management companies. Flo had always been very supportive of me, but I think I'm right in saying that the rest of Kerb weren't as keen, purely on account of me being so very new. She had seen me die on my arse at the Latitude New Act competition and sent me a message later saying she really liked my act and to stay in touch. I was impatient, though, and when she hadn't made an offer to sign me, I took the deal on the table with Lisa Thomas Management.

A year or so had passed and I was still unhappy with LTM. I decided I wanted to leave and if I then couldn't get an agent it would be a clear sign that I should probably be thinking about giving up. LTM replied, saying they

Above: Mum and Dad getting married, unaware this would lead to the creation of a legend. I mean me.

Left: At this stage it looked like both my eyes might be lazy.

Below: As a baby I had the uncanny ability to always look battered.

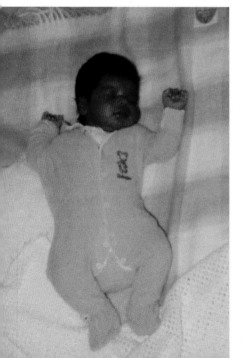

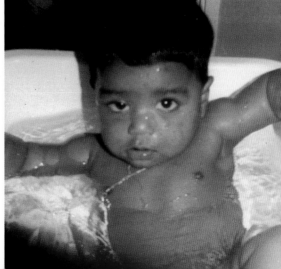

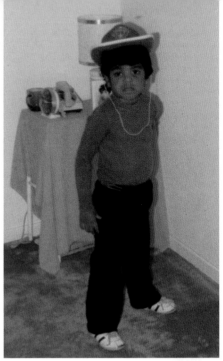

Left: I was so thick as a child my dad had to give me lessons in blowing out candles.

Above: My parents made me wear this hat to see if I could survive bullying.

My brother and I often used to play a game on holiday called 'Who can look the biggest loser?'.

Above left: There were other people at this party, honest.

Above right: My first crush, Sarah Elliot, being seduced by my hips.

Left: Whenever I see myself in this photo, my virginity grows back.

Above: Me with a drama prize I won at school. I appear to be playing the part of 'child who dresses like such a twat he has no friends'. I was pretty good in that role.

Below: Me with 'the crew' at school, aged fourteen. Shortly after this photo was taken they beat the shit out of me.

Left: My mum paid for us to have a series of family photos taken through the years. Amazingly, this is the best one.

Below: This was me on the way to work during my LSG Sky Chefs days. This car park is where my brother and I apprehended a joyrider.

Bottom: In my teaching days. This is me begging my mum to drop me off down the road from school – being taken to work by your mum as a teacher is a career-ender.

Above: My early comedy days. This is me at Always Be Comedy in Kennington, trying new material whilst blissfully unaware that the shirt I'm wearing really highlights sweat.

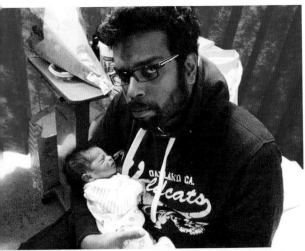

Left: Juggling two careers and a young family was tough, but I still found time for my many hobbies, such as holding tiny babies while looking as sinister as possible.

Below: Every time I'd do a big gig or make a TV appearance it would appear in the Crawley papers, which is a damning indictment of how much is going on in the town.

Above: On tour with Kevin Bridges and doing the 'we're surprised by breakfast' face.

Right: Selfie during walk from hell on *Asian Provocateur*. This kid thought I was such a wuss.

Below right: Shitting myself before a rap performance in Sri Lanka for *Asian Provocateur* – it did not go well.

Below left: With my cousin Pratheep on *Asian Provocateur 2*. This is just before some rednecks asked me to shoot semi-automatic weapons with them.

Above left: Me with the two most important women in my life (just kidding, Mum) – my agent Flo, and Leesa.

Above right: My attempt at making Leesa and me look hip hop. She insists on keeping a seat between us at all times.

Left: This is me teaching our youngest child a harsh lesson about favouritism.

were disappointed but understood. They had spoken to Phil McIntyre Entertainments, the promoters of my Edinburgh show, who had decided they could no longer promote it. This was less than ideal just a couple of months before Edinburgh and it wasn't helping my throwing the dice and letting fate decide my future. It took a couple of weeks, but I was able to find new promoters in Matthew Harvey and Live Nation. About the same time, Flo had a chat with me after a gig and I opened up and explained how unhappy I had been and that I was struggling to see a future in comedy. She was very sympathetic, and with her help we salvaged my Edinburgh show: *Rom Com*.

Just before I left LTM I was seriously considering stopping stand-up. We were completely broke and I was travelling all over the country to do gigs for no money and coming home to not pay the bills. It was depressing. I had just gone to Glasgow to do a gig and I was getting the train to Leicester to compete in the *Leicester Mercury* Comedian of the Year competition. This was part of the Leicester comedy festival, in which promoters would submit acts who had impressed them during the year. I had been put forward by Darrell Martin. I phoned Leesa from Glasgow in a state of defeat. I had no idea why I was continuing to do comedy but I was going to do the competition, then have a serious think about what the bloody point was. I thought Leesa was starting to feel the same. There is only so long you can carry on in voluntary poverty and she was starting to get spontaneously teary, which I always think isn't a great sign in a marriage.

It was this decision to sack it all off that liberated me

from any pressure to do well. I felt no nerves at all going into the competition. I was up against some great acts, including . . . I won't name them – it's not their bloody story, is it?

I won the competition – which was something of a hollow victory anyway, because I was criticized by some people for being too experienced to enter. What was so important, though, was the timing. I had arrived convinced I was going to walk away from stand-up, then this competition convinced me to keep going. This paragraph is sickening, isn't it? That night, I learned that the greatest competition of all is with yourself.

Not really, I'm just taking the piss.

Shortly after the *Leicester Mercury*, I was desperately gathering material together for my show in Edinburgh when I did 'Old Rope', the new-material event run by Tiff Stevenson. A piece of rope hangs onstage, and whenever you're doing old material you're supposed to hold on to the rope. It sounds terrible but it's one of the most popular new-material nights among comics and you always get really good people doing it. The comedians usually gather at the back of the room. I get on with most comics, but there are very few I would consider friends. I would also go as far as to say I find groups of comics borderline unbearable. One of the reasons I don't enjoy the Edinburgh Festival is because I find walking through town and bumping into loads of comics talking about shows as appealing as the idea of making the floor of our shower mirrored. I don't think it helps that I've always been married with kids when I've been doing comedy and usually keen to leave gigs and get home, but it also doesn't help that socially I expend very little effort, which is a pretty clear sign of a shit human.

That particular night I arrived and made my way to the back of the room, where I was greeted by a group of comics. One of them, who I will refer to as 'Douchebag', got up and started what felt like a routine where he showed me around, explaining where the comics sat and what the night was. I felt he was doing it for the benefit of the group, and had no idea why, but he was obviously enjoying the role-play. I sat down, and tried to ignore him. But every time I spoke, Douchebag did some patronizing chat to the effect that I wasn't to know how things worked. Eventually I asked what the hell he was on about, and one of the other comedians let me know that Douchebag was making a point about me entering the *Leicester Mercury* competition despite the level of my experience. And he had a point. Rob Beckett, who is in my 'comedy year group' did the competition three years before me in 2010, and Matt Rees, the brilliant comic who won in 2012, the year before me, was far less experienced than I was. I was still annoyed. The fact that it was explained to me suggested they had been talking about it before I arrived and Douchebag had decided to make me an unwitting participant in his bit. I don't know Douchebag that well and I was fairly pissed off about it.

That night I felt like the unpopular kid at school. Douchebag was hosting, and as he brought me up I was so angry I contemplated venting in my act about what had gone on. Now that I can see how pathetic the perceived slight was, I'm hugely relieved I didn't: I can't imagine anyone in the

audience would have given a shiny shit. As soon as I'd finished my set I left, deciding I never wanted to do another
night where I felt so unwelcome. I later realized I was
being a bit of a baby.

I do have a slight persecution complex. As soon as
somebody says something, I assume that everyone in that
group is in on the joke at my expense and I tar all of them
with the same brush. I remember supporting Seann Walsh
in Barnstaple. Luke Honnoraty, who ran the gig, asked if
we wanted to go out afterwards, which we did. We were at
a pub and I was smoking at the time. I was outside looking
for a light and asked a guy in a group if he had one. He
gave me his lighter, and as I went to spark up the cigarette,
he said, 'Aren't you going to say thanks?'

One of his friends said, 'Never mind thanks, he needs
to apologize for even being in this country.'

I was immediately angry, and wanted to tell the guy to
fuck off, but I was also aware that I didn't know the place
and any reaction would probably lead to my being beaten
up, so I made the cowardly decision to give back the lighter,
scowl at them, and walk away. Then I was struck by the
sudden thought that everybody at the pub was a racist.

Seann Walsh helped me survive during my early days of
comedy. We met very early on and he was very nice to me,
so I was delighted when he asked me to be his support act
for his tour. Being a support act requires a number of skills.
First and foremost, you must be able to drive, and navigate
effectively. I could drive, but my navigation was woeful. We
had many journeys of me instructing wrong turnings and
Seann asking me what the fuck was going on. Second, a

support act needs to be bearable for the main act to be around for long periods – something else I found challenging as I'm annoying to be around for any extended period. I believe that my being away from home so much is the main reason my marriage has survived. I tackled this with Seann by being relatively low-maintenance and not talking much. Finally a support act mustn't overlap material-wise with the main act, and not be so good as to make it difficult for him or her to follow. I was excellent at that.

Going on as the support act is hard, but it was the thing that improved me, possibly more than anything else. The audience are often not aware there is a support act, and even if they are, they won't have heard of you or particularly want to see you. You are a twenty-minute interruption to their evening.

Support acts can smash it, though. I once did a tour show in Andover and my regular support, Phil Jerrod, couldn't do the gig so Tom Allen very kindly stepped in. Tom is brilliant. He went on and absolutely killed it. People were going nuts. I was standing backstage, watching and enjoying, thinking I was about to have an amazing gig. But, as it turns out, Andover much preferred Tom Allen to me. I went on and started my show, and it became apparent very quickly that I was not going to be having the roof-smasher of a gig that Tom had had. What I was going to have was a group of people feeling nostalgic for that time when Tom Allen had done comedy for them. It was awful, compounded by the number of messages I got afterwards asking for details of the 'much funnier guy who supported you'.

In my head I imagined something similar happening for

me in my early days: walking onstage and people going, 'Who is this guy? We didn't know there was a support!' Then I start doing my set and people are laughing like maniacs and going, 'Oh, shit, this guy is amazing! How have I not heard about this dude? He is the best! Who the hell is Seann Walsh? We love this guy!' I certainly achieved the first part of that. I spent most of the first tour supporting Seann dying on my arse, with the only laughter coming from Seann, who found it hilarious. That made it a lot easier. Seann had been a support act and knew how tough it could be. He told me not to worry about how I was doing. Gradually, the gigs started to get easier and after one I even received a positive tweet, which I was irrationally happy about.

The money I made as Seann's support really kept us afloat. On top of that, Seann kept looking for ways to help me out. He was doing a show called *Stand up for the Week* on Channel 4, in which a group of comics would each do a set based on the news from the previous week, with each one covering a section like politics or sport. Seann had entertainment. One day, on the way to a gig, he asked me what topical gags I might come up with that week. I started riffing with him and we came up with a small routine. I can't be sure but I think he was seeing if I could write. And that short conversation convinced him I couldn't because he never broached it again.

A couple of weeks later, I was desperate to show him I could do it so I offered to write some jokes for nothing. And he accepted. He sent me the topics for the next episode and I wrote a load of material. He emailed back saying it was basically shit. The next week I sent him another load of stuff. He told me it was still shit but better than last time. I sent him another load of material, and he invited me in to do a day's trial as a writer, then had me on as a regular contributor. This was immense for me. Not only was I working in TV but the money I was making from writing was keeping my family fed and clothed. I can't tell you how grateful I was and still am to him. We'd had nothing, and suddenly we could make ends meet. Seann had not only allowed me to keep trying out for the show but, because I wasn't an official writer, he'd paid me out of his own pocket. I will never forget what he did for me.

His looking out for me didn't stop there. Once I had finished on *Stand Up for the Week* he did a show for Comedy Central and asked me to help on that too. Again the money was invaluable. The show had a press launch and they wanted a couple of comedians to perform. Seann asked me to do it. I did my set and thought nothing of it. But the show was produced by Open Mike, the same company that produces *Live at the Apollo*. I didn't realize they were booking for that show too.

Two weeks later I was with Leesa, dropping the boys at nursery, when my phone rang. It was one of the guys from Open Mike, contacting me directly because I had left Lisa Thomas Management. 'Is this Romesh? We were just wondering how you would feel about doing *Live at the Apollo*.' I couldn't believe it. Just a few months earlier I'd been contemplating giving up. It was the closest I've felt to the end-of-a-movie moment. I also knew that the money from doing *Live at the Apollo* would mean I didn't have to worry about paying the bills for a couple of months.

Around this time Flo contacted me to let me know that she had spoken to everyone at Off the Kerb and they were onboard with signing me. The only person left to convince was Addison Cresswell. This was problematic as he was the head of the company. I had only encountered Addison once, and that was when I was at an Edinburgh Awards ceremony: he approached me to say he'd got so out of it on Tuesday that he'd lost Wednesday. Or something. Anyway, he was a character.

This was further complicated by the fact that Flo had been banging the drum at the office for signing me, and Addison had just seen me deliver what he believed to be a dreadful set. Having done some writing for them, I had been invited to perform on the new series of *Stand Up for the Week*. It was episode two and apparently all of the acts had been edited except mine. Addison turned up at the edit, asked to watch everything and saw me deliver what he felt was an unacceptable set. He phoned Flo and told her how bad I was. She phoned me to have a chat about it. This had made the situation a lot more difficult.

Having been enraged by my perceived incompetence, Addison was then incredibly nice to me. He phoned me before the next episode to ask what I had material wise and offer advice. It was weird advice: he said things like 'Stop trying to be Paul Chowdhry,' which, while I love Paul, I was definitely not trying to do. He then came to the recording of the next episode to give me a pep talk. Addison was pure charisma, which had the effect of making him terrifying. He talked me through my set, reminded me not to be Paul Chowdhry and watched me perform. Afterwards he offered me a lot of encouragement about how I'd done, suggested that I might have come across as a bit homo-phobic, and told me to have a drink to celebrate. A few days later he called to let me know that he was in the edit and I was going to look bloody amazing. This was nice, but again I found the whole process terrifying. It also didn't matter how good I looked because, by this stage, only about seven people were watching *Stand Up for the Week*. But it had worked. A week later Flo called me to let me know we were on.

8.

It's Bigger than Hip Hop

I love hip hop so much. It's helped form my identity, seen me through years of being down and out, and has meant that my dress sense is a bit middle-aged-dad-trying-to-be-cool. I first got into hip hop when I was a kid and have never stopped listening to it, despite my wife's insistence that I should have grown out of it by now. My one sadness in my marriage is that I haven't managed to convert Leesa to hip hop. She hates it. HATES IT. It would have been easier to convert her to Islam. Which I'm trying next as a test.* Just this morning I was listening to Jurassic 5 in the kitchen while making breakfast. As soon as I stopped it, she threw her head back and said, 'Thank God for that.' That was Jurassic 5! Like, one of the most inoffensive rap groups around.

I wouldn't mind so much if she had a taste in music. I'm not saying she has bad taste, just that she barely has an opinion on it. She likes music she vaguely remembers as the background noise to her doing something else. She never actively listens to it. Which means whenever she has control of the car stereo, we have indie music on because

---

* I just want to point out that I'm not even Muslim. There's nothing wrong with it. I'm just not one. What a fucking minefield.

that's what was playing at that party when she got off with some bloke round the back of the Scout hut.

Until recently, my greatest success was taking her to a Roots gig and her saying she enjoyed it, but she hasn't sought out any more of their music. But then I made a breakthrough – not a great one, but a breakthrough nevertheless.

I'm an inconsiderate man. Not deliberately – I just don't have a particularly high regard for birthdays and anniversaries. I wouldn't care if everyone forgot my birthday, but I have to remember that not everybody else feels like that. This means that much of my life is spent apologizing to people for not remembering their latest milestone, and Leesa definitely bears the brunt of this. The advantage, for me at least, is that I have managed to lower her expectations to such a point that if she receives a card it's an achievement.

This year for our anniversary I remembered that she had mentioned wanting to see the musical *Hamilton*, and I booked up surprise tickets. Next-level husbanding. I told her we were going out, didn't tell her where, and when we arrived at the theatre she revealed she'd assumed it would be dinner and hadn't eaten anything all day. Because I'm Romesh Ranganathan, and I don't think things through properly.

I didn't hold out much hope for *Hamilton*. I'd been told by loads of people I'd love it because it was a musical with a hip hop soundtrack. That should have been right up my street, but I had visions of some dreadful appropriation of hip hop that would mean me spending the evening with loads of people talking about how amazing something was that took a massive dump all over my favourite thing.

It was actually incredible. This is not the place for a

Hamilton review, but the show was unbelievable and Leesa loved it. She even started to listen to the soundtrack in the car. My wife, actively seeking out rap music. My mind was blown. She still listens to it now. And I'm sick to death of it.

My early hip hop obsession had a major impact on my lifestyle: it encouraged me to dress like an imbecile. Back in my late teens I had some very special outfits. Me and the only other two guys at school who liked hip hop started wearing baggy jeans, headgear and thinking we were in Brooklyn. It was really bad. What made it worse was that we didn't know what we were doing. We would wear our interpretation of the look, like Asian knockoffs of an American product. In fact, I remember there was a gang of black lads from the other side of Crawley who would always laugh their tits off when they saw us doing an impression of them. When I look back on it, it was hugely embarrassing, but at the time I thought I was a proper G.

When I was in sixth form there was a girl I really liked called Natasha. I remember writing a rap for her. One of the lines went, 'Natasha you know you're not a ho or a bitch, and I want to let you know you turn me on like a switch.' I imagined Natasha showed the rap to her friends, saying, 'Isn't this romantic? Romesh says I'm neither a ho nor a bitch, and that I really turn him on, despite the fact he is a masturbating virgin.' I thought she was gorgeous but I never thought I'd have a shot with her.

Until one day we were in the common room and she started chatting and flirting with me. Oh my days! I couldn't believe it. I was throwing down all sorts of gags and chat, and she was laughing and playing with her hair.

I was smashing the convo. Then she told me she was going to the Base nightclub in East Grinstead later, and asked if I wanted to go too. *Holy shit, mate. Yes, I bloody do!*

The Base was the only nightclub in the area worth going to, and it was barely that. Everyone used to go there on a Friday and Saturday and there would be appearances from dance-music stars who had just started to go on the wane. I remember seeing Baby D there. But by the time I saw her she was probably Had Three Babies D. I was worried about making the right impression when I was out but I knew exactly what to do: go full rude-boy. I wore baggy jeans, smart shoes (because you couldn't get in with trainers), a baggy red shirt and a bloody waistcoat. I looked like Aladdin. The most amazing thing about that outfit is that I still haven't told you the worst part of it yet: I wore a bright red bandanna. What an absolute arsehole. I thought I looked like Tupac. What I actually looked like was Tupac just after he had auditioned to be in panto.

When I got to the club, Natasha took one look at me and headed off to another part of the venue. I was so deluded I decided this was part of a game to play it cool, so I decided not to chase. That meant I spent my night alone in a nightclub. I left without seeing Natasha, went to get a kebab, and a drunk girl told me she thought it was brave to wear a handkerchief out. After that Natasha and I didn't really talk again. Last I heard, she'd become a ho and a bitch, and very rarely, if ever, turned people on like a switch.

I was and am pathetic with women. I don't mean, as many comedians pretend onstage, that I'm shy and retiring, a nice guy just waiting for the right girl. I have never, ever,

ever pulled a girl at a nightclub. I have never had a one-night stand. And let me tell you why: I'm unattractive. And I'm not even the right unattractive. It's the lazy eye. Attractiveness is directly proportional to how symmetrical your face is. I can't even look in the same direction to tell you if something's symmetrical. Combine that with the physique of a man who is method-acting as a walrus and you really don't have much hope. I realize this all sounds like bollocks because I've found love. My wife is amazing and I'm very lucky. But she got to know me and we fell in love. If I'd approached Leesa in a nightclub or bar she wouldn't have given me the time of day. She denies it now because social convention dictates she has to.

It wasn't even like I had the chat when I did speak to a girl. I was twenty-five and had just split up with the girl I'd been seeing. A girl who, it transpires, had been cheating on me left, right and centre. I was trying to 'get back on the horse' and a friend of mine took me out, then spent the evening forcing me to approach women. We were at Ikon, a club in Crawley, which had a weird set-up with an American diner in the corner. Two girls were having something to eat, and my mate decided that they were to be our chat-up targets.

After much convincing I agreed to approach them, but had no idea what I was going to say. I walked up to one of the girls, having made up my mind that I wasn't going to chat her up but would simply engage her in polite conversation and see what happened. I thought I would just make an observation, but I didn't want to be cheesy, so I wouldn't say, 'You're fit.' Although that would probably have worked better than what I actually said. I noticed she was eating a hot dog and said, 'Looks like you're enjoying that.' How I didn't realize that would sound like I was suggesting she enjoyed blow-jobs is beyond me. She looked disgusted and turned away from me to talk to her friend, who was being spoken to by my mate, who couldn't believe I'd already managed to piss off my girl. When I told him what had happened, after he'd finished laughing he agreed not to pressure me into harassing any more girls. And I believe that's how I managed to get through my single years avoiding arrest.

Another time I'd just bought a white trench coat and thought I looked the dogs'. I was in Brannigan's in Crawley, a regular Tuesday hang-out for a while. Crawley is popular with lots of airport workers from Gatwick, so loads of the bars ran and still run a 'Hostie night' on Tuesdays, which means that Tuesday nights in Crawley look like Friday nights. So me and my 'crew' would go out on Tuesday, Friday and Saturday, every week without fail, for five or six years. And I did not pull once. You have to accept there was an issue there.

I was dancing in Brannigan's and there was a girl I thought was very attractive. I decided to try the traditional method of 'dancing behind a girl and seeing if she tells you to fuck off when she notices you'. And it worked! She glanced back and carried on dancing and I moved in closer and gave my mates the thumbs-up. About half an hour of this mating ritual continued until I thought it might be time to step it up a gear. I hadn't even spoken to her yet. I started to move in a bit closer to say hello. As I did this she turned and two things become apparent. First, she hadn't noticed me before. Second, now that she had, she was appalled. She looked at me in the same way that you might look at someone ugly who has been dancing behind you without you noticing for about half an hour. Wearing a creepy white trench coat. And as I had given the big thumbs-up to my mates, they had all witnessed what had followed. I was mortified.

I envy people who now have the internet to help them date – and I'm aware that makes me sound about a hundred. It seems to make things a lot less awkward. You can arrange dates without first having to do some sort of approach play. I'm terrible at reading signals. I could almost guarantee that every girl I approached was just trying to have a nice night with her friends without some goggle-eyed freak suggesting they're fellating a hot dog. I get that. Which is why I would have loved to have dating websites taking away all of the horror and allowing me to meet people based on interests and personality. I'm speaking from a position of complete ignorance here. Internet dating is a nightmare, according to the people I know who have done it, but it's got to be better than approaching someone cold, hasn't it? In fact, I think that should now be made illegal. Decriminalize marijuana and criminalize chirpsing.

The closest I've come to being on the receiving end of unwanted advances is being at the train station or the shops and seeing someone I know. The station is probably the worst, because there's no escape, and usually a pretty high chance that the person will then be on the same train as you, which means you have to sit next to them and have a dreadful conversation. I usually have a new album lined up to listen to on the train and I'm really keen to tuck into it, so my journey is ruined. Then as you part ways, you say something like 'We should meet up properly.' But as neither of you has bothered to meet up before this random encounter, it's probably a good sign that you shouldn't be friends. I'm pretty sure this awkwardness is felt on both sides, which is why I now try to avoid these situations at all costs.

I was at a tube station recently and somebody I went to school with was on the platform. I saw him, he saw me. That should have been it. We're not friends any more. We're strangers who happened to go to the same school. It was at least twenty years since I'd seen the guy, and that's enough time for stranger status to have grown back. This prick didn't think that so he came over and started talking. And then what do you say? 'How's it going? Do you think we'll have anything in common as adults? Could you please pretend to give a shit about my family situation and what I'm doing for a living?' We spoke for about two minutes, ran out of anything to say and stood in silence for the rest of the journey. The whole time I just wanted to say to him, 'Dude, you know this is your fault, right? We could have just nodded at each other and carried on with our day.'

Here's my solution to harassment. Nobody is allowed to approach anyone, but everyone has a set of cards with their interests and values on them, and a profile photo. It has to be just a headshot. It can't be some photo of you with an African kid by a well to show that you're a humanitarian. If you see a girl or a guy you like, you ask if you can give them a card, and then you leave them alone. You don't talk, you don't ask if you can circumvent the process and chat to them now, you don't mention the hot dog they're eating: you leave them alone. If and when they're ready they can contact you and ask why you think it's okay to wear a trench coat indoors. That's the solution.

I'm not blaming hip hop for my inability to pull, but I don't think it helped. There never seemed to be any girls at hip hop gigs (that's certainly not the case now) and there was something very nerdy and virginal about being an uncool hip hop fan, particularly back then. I originally started listening to Public Enemy and then moved on to NWA, Ice Cube and ICE-T, before broadening my tastes to stuff like De La Soul and the whole Native Tongues collective. Despite my occasional west-coast dalliances, I was basically an east-coast hip hop fan and I got pathetically into it. I would dress like a rapper, walk like a rapper, and I even started writing rhymes at school with a mate. It was all pretty embarrassing. I would say probably the highlight in terms of cringe was when I stole a VW badge and started wearing it on a shoelace around my neck.

I kept writing rhymes and having occasional battles with one of the other hip hop heads from school. I think even we knew it was shit, but we couldn't get enough of it. I loved everything about it – collecting the tapes, the dancing, the culture. I used to read and write into *Hip Hop Connection* magazine religiously. My most embarrassing letter, which ended up getting published, was all about how awful Snoop and Dre were, and how much I preferred

Tim Dog – a symptom of my east-coast obsession getting the better of me.

My own rap 'career' started when I was at uni, where I created my stage persona, Ranga. I'd written some lyrics and was desperate to link up with a DJ and start chatting over his mixes. I hooked up with a couple of other guys, Sehmi and Avin, and we started performing at clubs with a DJ we'd met called Yattin. Truthfully, we were awful. Yattin was good, but we were surplus to requirements. If he was playing a rap record, who the hell wanted to hear us rapping? We were just creating a racket, shouting things like 'Yattin in the place. With Ranga and Sehmi. Yes!' It was so bad. But it was fun to be going to clubs and working towards something, however hopeless. We once tried to record some stuff but we were too lazy to write lyrics so it was just us repeating the same raps over and over on different tracks.

One night we even got attacked, although I'm placing the blame for that firmly at Yattin's door. We were at a small club in Kingston and Yattin decided to play a track by Brand Nubian, the beginning of which is a sample of the Muslim call to prayer. He can't claim to be surprised by this as the track is called 'Allah U Akbar'. Within seconds of the track starting, the booth was surrounded by Muslims, angry that we had played a call to prayer in a place where drink was served and all sorts of naughtiness was going on. I can't remember what calmed them down but, based on how the night had gone, I imagine we just promised to stop MCing.

I remember some of the lyrics I used to drop. Here's a little sample:

The basic way in which I bring that type of mayhem will only
*   become apparent to an MC when I slay him,*
Stay trim, my verbals ain't flabby, but these others come with
*   words like your girl; they're fucking shabby.*
I leave mic devices disassembled, you must worship when I spit,
*   my lyric is my temple,*
Most of these MCs come like Bee Gees when they test my vibe
*   cos while my object's victory,*
Their object is just Staying Alive,
Strive with combinations of chatter to break these rappers down
*   to denominations of natter,*
I'm like Rubik's cube these stupid dudes will never comprehend,
*   my complexity relies on my ability to transcend,*
Your basic metaphor, in semaphore I'm incredible, I'm extra
*   tasty with it while these others are inedible.*

It doesn't even make sense. How the hell do you test
somebody's vibe? And I must have been on the weed when
I decided that my complexity relied on my ability to transcend – I was essentially just shitting out a thesaurus. To be
fair, I am incredible in semaphore.

I once went to a hip hop and R&B night at my brother's
girlfriend's uni. It was a strange evening because *Pop Idol*
was really huge and the whole bar had been set up with the
final being shown on the big screen. The bar was half full
of people desperate to know the results of the final, and
half full of people dressed up for an R&B hip hop night
waiting for it to finish. I was slightly older, which I always
felt gave you an edge with the girls at those nights, although
obviously it wasn't enough to help me.

There's a point at which being older works to your advantage, and another at which you've peaked, and it's sad that you're still out cutting loose with a much younger crowd. I used to go to clubs a lot, and these weird older guys would turn up, most of whom looked like somebody's uncle. I couldn't work out why they continued to come out, unless they really got off on making people feel slightly uncomfortable.

Then I found myself out one night, glancing in a mirror and coming to the realization that I now looked like one of the creepy guys. I remember saying it into the mirror in the club toilets – the site of many of my epiphanies, or what some might call breakdowns. Every so often I'll be drunk in a toilet, washing my hands, and catch myself in the mirror, then just monologue to myself about what an idiot I am: 'You're drunk, mate. Everyone knows it. Why do you have to get so drunk? You're pathetic. They're not your real friends out there, you know. They think you're an idiot too. And you're fat. And your eye's so messed up you can't even look at yourself in the mirror properly. You're a joke, mate.' And then I head back to the bar to get more drinks.

To be fair, drunk me has a valid point about the eye. It's essentially my personal version of a breathalyser. It becomes more off centre and droopy the more drunk I get. If it shuts completely, it's time to get my stomach pumped. Anyway, one day I went into a nightclub toilet, and Mirror Romesh and I decided we couldn't go clubbing any more.

The *Pop Idol* final finished and the night started properly. The DJ started playing banger after banger and the crowd were going nuts. Then the DJ got on the mic and asked if there was anyone who could rap. Hello, pricks, here is Ranga's opportunity to shine. Immediately – and drunkenly, as I was really happy about Will Young winning *Pop Idol* – I stepped up to the booth and volunteered my services. The DJ handed me the mic, and I began to spit pure fire. Oh my God, mate, it was incredible. I was doing written verses and these were getting *8 Mile* style cheers from the crowd, and then I ran out of written stuff so I started freestyling and it went up a notch. The crowd were going nuts. It was nearly impossible for me to really focus on the rapping as I was so distracted by the thought of how much sex I was going to be having as a direct result of this performance. The only decision left to make was not to overstay my welcome.

I dropped my final bar to the crowd going wild. I handed the microphone to the DJ, who hugged me in admiration, and then I tripped and fell all the way down the stairs from the DJ booth in full view of everyone. The one thing I'm grateful for is that the DJ didn't stop the track. I stood up immediately, and realized two things: one, I had quite badly injured my ankle, and two, I couldn't let anyone know that I had injured my ankle. I spent the rest of the night smiling and dancing while trying not to cry, and telling everyone who asked that the fall hadn't hurt as badly as it looked. I felt like Madonna.

I've had weird experiences at nightclubs. I once went with a girlfriend and her mates to Clapham Grand for a seventies night and was accosted by the lollipop dude in the toilets. I've always felt these guys don't get the recognition they deserve. I've lost count of the number of nights they've helped me remember 'No splash, no gash'. That particular guy took a real shine to me because I was the only other person of colour he had encountered the whole night. He started telling me how excited he was to see me, and that brothers needed to stick together. He even refused to take any money from me even though I'd 'freshened up for the punani'. It breaks my heart that so many of our younger generation no longer bother to do that.

And so it was all night. Every time I went in there, he gave me everything for free. It felt great to have a toilet ally. The final time I went in, I found all of the lollipops and after-shaves out, but my new BFF was nowhere to be seen. I stood in front of the stuff and decided to wash my hands and leave, when I heard my friend say, 'Help yourself to whatever you need, my brother.' I looked around to see where he was and was horrified to see he was in one of the cubicles, sitting on the toilet with his pants down and with the door wide open so he could keep an eye on the stuff. He asked me about my night. I wanted to tell him it had been going great until social etiquette had forced me to engage in a conversation with a man who was taking a shit, but I decided I didn't want to add any more awkwardness to my new friendship.

It was also ridiculously easy to get into fights in those clubs. I remember being at Rainforest Café one night, standing in the corner of the bar while my mates bought drinks. It seems unusual that everyone except one person would go to buy drinks, and I'm now thinking I may have been the group outcast, but that's something for me to discuss with my counsellor. I was standing on my own, and a group of lads barged past me, in a manner you had to get used to at those nights. There was no point picking people up on it, because you'd just get started on. One guy at the back, though, actively shoved me as he walked past. He turned around, gave me a look, then gestured to his phone. I looked at it as he started to write a text message, which I realized was for me to read. He typed: 'I am deaf, but don't let that make you think you can mess me about. I will fuck you up' – something like that.

I wasn't sure of the etiquette. Was I supposed to read the message and give him a thumbs-up to confirm he didn't have to fuck me up? Was I supposed to type a response into his phone? As it turned out, it didn't matter, because what he decided to do was scream into my face like a lunatic. I wasn't sure how to respond, and then all of his friends came running over. I thought I was going to get a genuine pasting. In fact, they had come to usher him away and explained to me he was deaf. I told them it was fine and that in future he could probably save that text message as a template to avoid having to type it out each time.

Growing up on a council estate made this sort of insane situation feel quite familiar. When I was sixteen, I went to see a mate and he told me he had beef with some bloke on the next road. I can't remember what the issue was, but I'm sure it was incredibly important. Maybe he'd taped over his Shabba Ranks album or something. Anyway, he asked me if I would back him up as he confronted the guy.

'Backing someone up' is something I've done a lot of in my time. Essentially it means standing behind them and looking hard while inside you cry and hope to God a fight doesn't actually break out. Of course I agreed. There was no option, really, but I was also exceptionally good at standing behind someone, provided a fight didn't actually take place, in which case my only real use would have been to provide a human shield. I got my game face on and we both walked to where this guy was hanging out. He was bigger than either of us, and I was pretty sure he could take both of us so I was really hoping that this didn't kick off. My friend started asking this guy why he'd been bad-mouthing him, and the guy was denying it. Pretty standard stuff for a council-estate stand-off in Crawley. The thing that worried me, though, was that the guy didn't seem to be backing down, and neither did my mate, which meant there was a good chance this would turn into an actual fight.

I tried to counteract this by increasing my level of backing up, which meant looking annoyed at what was being said, throwing my arms up and occasionally spitting. This did nothing. Then my friend opened his jacket and pulled out what can only be described as a small sword. There were two things to process here: first, this had escalated the situation, and second, this was a pretty damning indictment of my backing-up abilities. It seemed to have the desired effect: the other guy immediately freaked out and went to run away, whereupon my mate started chasing him, shouting things like 'That's it, run away, you pussy,' as if running away from a teenager with a sword was anything other than incredibly sensible. If anything, we should have been shouting, 'That's it! Follow basic-survival instinct, you non-suicidal idiot!' We chased the bloke off, and my mate decided to take the sword back to his house before we continued with our day, which I concurred was absolutely the best thing to do.

We had just returned the sword to his bedroom and were walking along the street talking about how good I'd been at backing him up, when a car screeched to a halt next to us. The doors opened and our sword runner and three of his mates got out of the car brandishing golf clubs. We glanced around. There was nowhere to run. We looked at each other as if to say, 'Okay, we're going to get beaten up with golf clubs now.'

It was very much like the end of *Toy Story 3* when they're headed for the furnace, except we didn't hold hands. I was just putting my arm up to protect myself from the first blow when I heard, 'Oh my God, it's Romesh!' I looked from behind my arms to see that one of the guys who was about to beat the shit out of us was the boyfriend of a mate of mine. 'I'm sorry, mate, I can't beat up Romesh. This is done. See you later, Rom.' The backing-up gods had sent me a blessing!

I'd gone on to do my master's (the one where I left my exam paper blank) and was preparing to leave my hip hop dreams behind me when I bumped into an old mate from school as I was waiting for a tube. I knew he'd gone into music production but he mentioned that he was now doing a lot of hip hop stuff. We exchanged details and I arranged to go round to his and lay down some lyrics.

A few weeks later I turned up at his place. He was there with a DJ called Dough and we got ready to put down a track. This was nerve-racking for me: although I'd told him

I could rap, I hadn't actually done it in front of either of them. There was a good chance that they would be trying not to crack up laughing. They didn't laugh and I have no idea how good they thought I was, but Dough and I started doing some bits and pieces and he got me together with another rapper called Wormz. There was no plan, no ambition and, I would argue, no desire in any of us to take things further. We would just occasionally meet up, rap a bit and I'd go home with the tape thinking I was a rapper.

A few months later I saw an ad in *Hip Hop Connection* looking for battle rappers for something called Battle Scarz – essentially an *8 Mile*-style competition. They were looking for rappers to send in tapes so they could choose entrants for a competition that was taking place at Scala in King's Cross. I recorded some rhymes, sent them in and was selected to compete. I went along with a few mates, unprepared for what I was to be involved in. The gig was mad: it was absolutely heaving with hip hop fans, and they were all rowdy as anything. I walked in and was almost immediately crippled with nerves.

The first round involved us rapping over a beat we had preselected and brought with us. I had burned mine onto a CD and the disc failed, cutting out just at my killer punch line, which actually helped: I got through.

The second round was a simple *8 Mile*-style battle. You had to take turns to go at each other for thirty seconds each, then the judges and crowd would decide a winner. It was horrendous. People were doing throat-slit gestures and telling you that you were going to choke as you walked onstage. Luckily, I was up against somebody who just couldn't do it.

It was almost as if someone had rigged things in my favour. I delivered thirty seconds of turgid dogshit and then he, against all odds, managed to serve up something worse.

The third round involved a band. You had to give them the elements of the track beatbox style and they would re-create them for you to rap over. By this stage, I knew I was out of my depth, so my strategy was to have a catchy enough beat that would carry through the lacklustre lyrics. So I basically did the beat to 'Billie Jean'. This in combination with an opponent who was, again, next-level incompetent meant that I was through to the final.

You know when England get knocked out of an early round of the World Cup, and then you're watching a team they would have played later in the tournament mullering somebody and you think, Christ, I'm glad we're not play-ing them? Well, imagine that scenario, except England get through and are obliterated to the extent that they have to leave wearing burqas. That is essentially what happened to me in the final.

It was me versus two guys in a battle to the death. They were both excellent and deserved to be there, and as soon as we started, the other two immediately saw there was a runt in the litter. They turned on me to eliminate me as quickly as they possibly could. I cannot tell you how awful it was to feel the crowd smell blood. It was like the Colosseum. I tried to retaliate by dropping the worst freestyled rhyme heard in a while: 'Here I am spitting bars in the Scala, You can't handle the heat of my chicken tikka masala.' Fucking hell. I mean, literally the mildest curry you can get on the whole menu. I was doomed.

Talking of tikka masala, my dad used to have a theory that white people got treated better in Indian restaurants. This meant he had a huge chip on his shoulder whenever we went to one. We used to go to an Indian restaurant in Crawley. One night we were in there and my dad was convinced we were hurried to our table while all the white people were getting their butts kissed and their shoes shined. The waiter came over to take our order and my dad said, 'Does this dish come with rice?'

The waiter replied, 'Yes, it comes with rice, you know.'

Dad blew up: 'No, I don't fucking know. If I knew, why the hell would I be asking you?' He might have had a point but his reaction felt disproportionate to the waiter's actions. I also thought we ran the risk of some extra phlegm in the biryani.

That still wasn't my most embarrassing experience in an Indian restaurant. That award goes to the time when I was touring with Suzi Ruffell and we used to hit up a curry house after every show. One night we arrived at a restaurant and ordered. I was necking beers and suddenly needed a piss. I went off to have one, then returned to the meal. As Suzi was talking to me, I suddenly felt a warmth in my genital area. I wasn't sure if I was imagining it, but soon it was a deeply uncomfortable burning. Somehow I had transferred jal farezi spice to my dick*. I made my excuses and ran to the toilet. I tackled the issue as best I could, then returned to the table where I had no choice but to

---

* I have since been informed that this is a common complaint known as 'chilli willy'.

explain what had happened to Suzi, who was partly laughing but mostly appalled at my over-sharing.

I was ejected from the rap battle after the masala line, the audience really hating me now. My friends walked ahead because the crowd's vitriol was so brutal. I even had guys offering to battle me because they thought it was an easy win. And then, just as I was leaving, I noticed Mike Skinner among them, and my exit from hip hop was complete. I never rapped again. Seriously, at least. Sadly, every interview I have ever done has involved me being asked to perform some sort of rap but, in the main, I have avoided it. In my version of *8 Mile*, Eminem would have gone 'Actually it turns out you're right – I'm not cut out for this.'

From that point on I decided to be a hip hop consumer only. I've carried on going to gigs, buying the music and dressing like a prick, though. For a while I was obsessed with Nas and in 2005, me, my brother and a mate managed to get tickets to see him in Brixton. We were buzzing as we went in. Then about thirty minutes into the show I was slightly separate from the other two when I heard a loud bang. I assumed it was a sound effect or some technical issue, but another couple of bangs made it obvious it was a gun. People were flipping out and running for the exits, screaming. My brother told me his enduring memory of the incident would be me zigzagging across an empty space in the venue, providing a clear target for any gunman requiring one.

As we made our way to the doors, Nas came out and said something along the lines of 'You think a gun is going to stop me?' The remaining crowd tried to get into it, but the gunshots had put a bit of a dampener on the whole thing.

Nas carried on, then brought out Dizzee Rascal for a bit. I say a bit: Nas never came back. So I guess what he meant was: 'Do you think a gun is going to stop me? Well, yes, it is, but not before I put Dizzee Rascal in the line of fire.'

One of the things that I've been so grateful for is that my comedy career has allowed me to participate in hip hop in my own way. It all started in Camden by accident. Rob Beckett and I were taking part in the Camden Fringe festival back in 2011. We were performing in a show run by Rupert Majendie. (If you listen to my Hip Hop Saved My Life podcast, you will know him as the now legendary RuMaj, but back then he was the mere mortal Rupert.) He ran, and still does, a live comedy company called Knock-2Bag. Rupert was also a producer for the BBC and was one of the first people involved in that world to take an interest in working with me.

One of the first projects we decided to make was essentially a sketch based around a bit of stand-up I was doing at the time about Froot Loops breakfast cereal. It was pretty revolutionary stuff. The short essentially involved me delivering my material to the camera with some acted-out scenes. We were shooting it at a studio in north London, and there was a scene where I went to Kellogg's offices and demanded to know why they didn't sell Froot Loops in the UK. This was based on a true story: I went to Canada, fell in love with Froot Loops, then wrote a complaint letter to Kellogg's. That I had the time to do this tells you everything you need to know about my life at that stage.

We decided to step out of the studio and pretend one of the offices on the site was Kellogg's. They set up the cameras and I started banging on the door of the empty office, demanding answers. I was in full flow when I heard a man scream, 'What the fuck are you doing?' and come sprinting down some stairs nearby. He was carrying a weapon and ran towards me, brandishing it – I'm pretty sure he thought I was trying to break in – but then he saw the cameras and realized what was going on. He already had a lot of adrenalin in his system.

'What the hell are you doing?'

'We're just, er, filming something for the BBC.'

'Do you have permission to be shouting and banging on doors?'

'Well, we've just hired one of the studios and we thought it would be okay . . .'

'It's not fucking okay. Right, you're not allowed to leave until someone at the BBC gives me two thousand pounds. Steve [the security guy], do not let any of these people leave unless I say so.'

What had initially started as a pleasant afternoon filming some substandard comedy had led to us becoming hostages. We went inside and had a conversation about who was going to speak to the BBC to arrange the money for our release. Rupert phoned up the guy we had booked the studio with. He said, 'Oh, that's Chris. He's a bit like that.' *A bit like that!* That's what you say about somebody who can be a tad grumpy or doesn't like mornings, not a guy who recreates a low-budget version of *Die Hard*.

You'll be delighted to know that we eventually negotiated our release but, sadly, the classic Froot Loops material never saw the light of day.

When Rob and I turned up to the venue in Camden, the plan was for Rob to compère the first part, then bring on comedians as they showed up. I was due to compère the last section at the end of the night, with a few other comics keeping things running in between. The problem Rob faced was that the bar was empty. When he asked Rupert what we should do, Rupert suggested starting and people would come in, which is in the top five of the shittest ideas I've ever heard. Rob rightly pointed out that doing crowd work to an empty room might look absolutely mental.

When I came back later that night to do my stint, I was faced with a very different scene. Liam Williams was hosting and doing a great job, but the crowd was descending into drunken madness. They were shouting over acts and starting chants. It was like doing comedy to a group of people who had come to watch the football. I walked up to Rupert and asked him what the hell we were going to do. He said we needed to do a spot of crowd control, so we decided to do a hip hop comedy set. This involved me going up and starting jokes with a punchline that was a hip hop tune title and playing it. For example: 'I was working at a shop and I was going through the complaints box. There were nearly a hundred. A customer walked in and said, "Please could you feed my dog? She's pregnant." And I said, "I feel bad for you, son. I got ninety-nine problems and a bitch ain't one."' Then we'd play the song. Now I've typed it out it seems awful, but on the night it worked perfectly. That was the beginning of Rupert and me trying to combine comedy with hip hop.

We finally settled on a podcast: *Hip Hop Saved My Life*.

We didn't have any aspirations for it at all. We just knew loads of comics who liked hip hop so we thought we'd chat to them about it, and that a format would emerge. Our first guest was Mark Smith, who is obsessed. We met at Rupert's office, recorded the podcast on a laptop and put it out. And got literally zero feedback. That may have been why we didn't put out another episode for about eight months, but once we started getting into a rhythm we put them out more regularly, and I've been amazed by the response.

What this meant, though, was that because the podcast was getting listeners, hip hop artists wanted to come on to promote their music. This was mind-blowing for me, and I got so bloody excited when Chali 2na from Jurassic 5 joined us for an episode, the only problem being that whenever I'm around people I really admire I lose my head. The biggest triumph of all this is that I feel like I'm participating in hip hop in my own small way without shitting on the culture by rapping terribly. It's been very cathartic.

9.

Can't Tell Me Nothin'

I am not happy with my first appearance on *Live at the Apollo*. I know other comedians who have similar memories of the shows that gave them their first big break on TV, but I was pretty destitute when I did that show. I wasn't as poor as I had been, but I certainly didn't have enough money for decent clothes – which is why, when you watch that *Apollo*, you will see that everything I'm wearing either doesn't fit or is shit. Even my hair looks like I'd smeared it with pig fat.

The weird thing is that I'm wearing much the same outfit on the other two occasions I've done *Apollo*, the difference being that by then I could afford decent versions so the clothes actually fit me. Every time a clip is shown from that first *Apollo*, though, I cringe. Appearances aside, I'm really not happy with my set. I get incredibly critical of my material very quickly and that set in particular shows me I wasn't ready to do that show. Don't get me wrong, I was glad to have done it, and the money helped, so I don't regret it. I just think I wasn't good enough for such a big gig.

I remember turning up on the day and having my photo taken next to the big *Apollo* sign, and then you have a picture taken with the other comics you're on with – in my case, Sean Lock and Marcus Brigstocke. I thought Sean and Marcus looked so bloody chilled, and that made me even more nervous. As it turned out, many people watching the show actually thought I was Marcus Brigstocke browned up, so perhaps I managed to channel some of his confidence. And hopefully that's more of an insult to him than it is to me. I felt so out of my depth and couldn't believe I was at the Apollo. I got taken to a dressing room and I just sat there shitting myself. I knew my set backwards, so there was no need to practise or prepare. I was just able to sit there and work up a sweat.

I don't get nervous any more. I hope I do well, but I don't get that horrible adrenalin-y feeling you get when you think you won't be able to go through with something. But at *Apollo* that night I had it so bad I was freaking out. I did the opposite of what you're supposed to do: I repeatedly visualized it going horribly wrong. When we were downstairs Sean Lock noticed and asked if I was okay. It was so weird. Everything I had done in comedy had been working towards moments like this and I wanted it so much, and now I was worried that the very desire to do it well would make me do it really badly.

You're allowed to request your walk-on music for *Apollo*, and I asked for 'Fix Up Look Sharp' by Dizzee Rascal because I thought it would make me feel like a badman. I suppose it worked to some extent, but I stood behind that big garage door that lifts up as you get introduced, and I shat myself some more. As the door began to open, I was convinced I wouldn't be able to remember how to speak. It was rank. However, with those sets, if you manage to get the first joke out and get a laugh, then everything else is a breeze. The trickiest bit is the first thirty seconds when you're not sure how it'll go. It went okay, I think, all things considered, but I'm still not happy with it.

Even in the short time between me doing my first and second *Apollo*, my attitude had changed and I had gained confidence. For my second appearance, I felt looser and much more relaxed. My main worry seemed to revolve around the fact that I wasn't worrying as much as I should be.

As I started to gain more TV experience, the only times I used to get nervous regularly were when I was doing *Mock the Week*, probably because I had an absolute shocker during one of the shows. My first appearance had gone okay – I was doing it with two really good friends, Rob Beckett and Josh Widdicombe, both of whom had done it before. They were very supportive – and Dara, Hugh Dennis and Andy Parsons were great too. The second featured Rob again, and Susan Calman was on. I felt all good mentally and was buzzing to get the second show under my belt, but from then on it was a disaster.

When you're doing that sort of show, they typically record for two hours plus. *Mock* is closer to three. So what you have to do is just go for it for the whole recording and see what happens. When it's edited down, you have seven people in a half-hour show, so you're not going to be saying loads in the final cut. What you're doing is just throwing gags out there and seeing if anything sticks. When you get more experienced two things happen: (a) more stuff tends to stick, and (b) you don't get fazed if it doesn't. Basically this means that if you say something that tumbleweeds, you need to get over it. On that particular night, Susan was doing some sort of story about cats, and just as she finished, I jumped in with a zinger. I say a zinger, but the thing stank out the room like a chemical weapon. It was like a black hole of laughter, sitting in the middle of the studio and sucking all laughter into it like a Death Eater. You get the idea. Anyway, if that happened now I would probably just say, 'Fuck, that was bad!' and we'd all move on. That night, because I was a bit green or whatever, I dropped the turd, everybody moved on and I sat there mortified.

The internal monologue from that point was my worst enemy. Rob was riffing about something and in my head I could hear a voice going, 'You've really fucked up there, mate. That was awful.' Then, for a few minutes, every time I thought about speaking, the voice would go, 'Nope—that's not funny enough, Romesh. Think of something else.' Eventually I said something that didn't play to complete silence and we moved on.

When we left the studio Flo was in the green room. She said, 'Do you want to have a chat?'

We went to my dressing room where she confirmed what I had feared: 'Were you okay out there? Because you said something that didn't go over and then you didn't say a single word for the next hour!' FUCKING HELL. I had become an elective mute for an hour! Holy shit. Flo reassured me that I had done enough for the edit and not to worry about it. Which I didn't. Much. To be honest, I really am a firm believer that things happen for a reason, so I assumed there was a good chance I wouldn't get asked back onto the show and made my peace with it.

A few days later I was driving to a gig when I got a phone call from Dan Patterson, the exec producer and creator of *Mock the Week*. 'Romesh, you were great the first time you came on, what the hell happened?' It was a horrible confirmation of what I'd suspected, but I was really grateful for the call. I'd assumed that if they thought I'd had a bad show they would simply delete my number and ignore me if I ever saw them in the street. I explained that I'd had a bad run where I was worried about saying anything. Dan reassured me: 'Look, we're going to get you back on, but don't do what you did last time!' On paper that looked like a real hospital pass. Because the next time I was on *Mock* I'd have to have a bloody great one. I'd buckled under the pressure last time when I hadn't been given an ultimatum.

That wasn't how I ended up reacting, though. I felt like Dan had given me an extra life. I was expecting not to be asked back and then, all of a sudden, they'd said, 'Give it one more bash.' So I did. I realized that being super-relaxed and chilled was the way to go. I sat back with not a care in the world because I hadn't expected to be there again, and the show went great. I say great: I never truly feel anything goes great, but I do experience moments of relief if something doesn't go completely shit, and that was how I felt. From then on I vowed to do everything as if it didn't matter. And that has served me well. Bar the times it has genuinely gone shit.

After that I started to do a lot of *Mock the Week*s. I hadn't realized how much of an effect it would have on my profile. I turned up to a student gig with Charlie Baker and Suzi Ruffell, both incredible comics and friends of mine, and it was my first experience of people wanting to have photographs taken with me because they'd seen me on TV.

Afterwards, I was driving back to Crawley when I noticed a car that seemed to be sticking really close to me. Every time I changed lane, the car would follow, and when I sped up it would speed up with me. It started to freak me out a bit, but I thought I might be imagining it, so I pulled into the slow lane and brought the car down to a dangerously low speed. I think I must have been doing about thirty. And now so was the fucking maniac who was tailing me. I started to have clear visions of being butchered and left by the side of the motorway.

I decided to come off at the next exit, figuring that if somebody was going to kill me, they probably wouldn't bother if they had to take a detour. My plan was to take the exit, go really slowly round the roundabout for a bit, then rejoin the motorway after they'd buggered off. I took the exit and did exactly that, but as I made my way down the slip road I saw that the murderer had slowed down and was waiting for me.

It was at this point that I accepted I was going to die. I became depressed that I was too old to be described as tragically young when I was found at the edge of the motorway. I started wondering why I never carried a weapon in the car, then decided I was so physically pathetic that a weapon would simply provide the attacker with something else to kill me.

As I pulled out in front of the waiting car, he or she (I fully respect the equal suitability of women to be serial-killers) changed lane and sped off. My relief was all encompassing. I also felt slightly offended, as if they had seen me as I was driving back onto the motorway and decided they didn't want a brown one. Or perhaps they'd recognized me from *Mock the Week*.

My questions were answered about five minutes later when I received a text from Charlie Baker, saying, 'You properly shit yourself, didn't you?' Which was a double whammy. Not only had he pranked me, but now lots of people, including Flo, who was also Charlie's agent, were going to know how pathetically terrified I was. They say you discover things about yourself in times of distress, and what I discovered was that my only survival technique was to go round a roundabout a few times, then step back into the killer's path because I didn't want to get home late.

Although I have had moments where things have suddenly taken an upturn, or one thing going well has led to loads of opportunities, I don't believe in make or break moments in your life. If you screw something up, it can knock you down, but that only means you'll be better when you get back to where you were before. Something like that. I also think luck has such a huge part to play. You can be good at comedy, which means people will take notice of you and you'll be given spots, but beyond that it really is luck that pushes you onto the next level. There are loads of brilliant comedians who haven't had the breaks, and plenty of average comedians who have. I don't think

I'm the best comedian they could have got for any of the things I've done. I'm fully aware that I'm very lucky, and if I ever forget that, I can just look at Twitter where I'll quickly find someone saying, 'Can somebody explain to me why somebody as unfunny as @RomeshRanga keeps managing to get on TV?' And then I feel the warm glow of knowing that my very existence is making that person angry. The rage might even shorten their life. I feel so fortunate.

The one thing that all ethnic-minority comedians seem to have to contend with is people telling them they talk about race way too much. This happens if they mention it at all. There are certain people who, when they see a female or an ethnic-minority comic, are basically waiting for them to mention something that they can accuse them of talking about all the time. For women it's periods and relationships, for ethnic-minority comics it's race. White male comedians don't seem to be subject to the same constraints.

I've talked about this with Rob Beckett, who said he joked about his teeth and being working class a lot, yet he'd never been accused of talking about either too much. I do try to work out whether an angle I have about race is interesting enough or funny enough to warrant inclusion, but the truth is I don't care. If a woman wants to go on about periods or I want to talk exclusively about race that should not be an issue. We should be letting market forces decide. If audiences stop laughing, you're probably talking too much about whatever it is, but if not, then it's nobody's right to pick you up on it. They can always go elsewhere.

There was one particular night on *Mock* when Hugh Dennis made an ISIS joke. I said it would have gone better if I'd laughed too so that people felt reassured. It became a running joke that every time somebody told a gag that had any connection with race, I would laugh loudly and everyone would feel better.

The night that show went out I got absolutely slaughtered on Twitter: '@RomeshRanga talking about race again. Quelle surprise'; '@RomeshRanga waited a whole two minutes before talking about his race.' I found it quite surprising and unfair. People seem to want a moratorium on anybody discussing anything that doesn't directly affect them, which means I'm being dictated to by people who have no direct experience of the subject I'm discussing.

I even had an ex-student do it. I was walking through a bar with a couple of friends when he tapped me on the shoulder. 'Hey, sir [all ex-students call you 'sir' for ever], loving your shows but just a little thing – drop the race stuff.' I was really pissed off. I didn't show it, just walked away, but I was extremely disappointed that somebody I'd taught had fallen into that trap.

I guess my position on the whole thing is this: if you can make all of my life experiences the same as a white guy's, and you can stop me experiencing racism, which I do all the time, then I'll stop talking about race. And if you have ever tweeted me or spoken to me suggesting I talk about it too much, that's a pretty racially intolerant position to adopt. Go fuck yourself.

To give you an example of the sort of thing I get, I just received this message on Facebook:

I seen ur program about Albania, it was very intentional
to make albania look bad,a u paki or smelly indian!!!

I seen many ptograms about your race,about Asian
gangs raping underage girls,maby you one of them!!!

If I'm receiving messages like that, surely I'm allowed to
do a joke or two with a head wobble, mate.

I owe Dan Patterson a lot. Because of that run of *Mock
the Week* shows, which wouldn't have happened had he not
given me another chance, my profile increased and my
Edinburgh show that year had almost sold out before I
arrived. This was a massive pressure off my shoulders, as
I now just had to do the show without worrying about
word of mouth or trying to get people in. All I had to do
was deliver an hour of material every night.

The other complication with my Edinburgh run was that
Leesa was pregnant with our third child and was due to
give birth during the festival. This was a huge issue as
there was no way I was going to miss the birth. I'm happy
to be negligent once the child is born, but I like to be there
at the start of its life. When I spoke to Leesa about it, she
seemed to think the easiest solution was to move the family with me and have the baby in Edinburgh. She had lived
there for a year previously and was convinced it would be
a doddle, so that was what we did.

That Edinburgh was a rollercoaster for me. Although I
had sold out my venue, the Pleasance Courtyard, I'd been
distracted by lots of bits and pieces of TV and radio so I
felt my show was undercooked. The first night of the festival felt like I was going into it with no real clue of what I

was doing, my set still a work in progress. Then I found out that a reviewer was in, namely Jay Richardson from the *Scotsman*.

I've arrived at a point now where I couldn't give a shiny shit about reviewers, but there's a time in your career when they're important to you, not just for the impact a good review can have on ticket sales, but also because it might encourage TV people to come and see you. Flo was keen to point out to me that I didn't need people to be encouraged to come, but I still felt a very real fear that reviews would be shit and people would return their tickets or, worse, they'd turn up in a dampened mood, giving me tougher crowds and a massive hurdle to overcome every night.

You know by now that I hate the Edinburgh Festival. It's been very good to me but I hate it. It's too middle class, it's too white, and it benefits everybody except the struggling acts it was supposed to be for in the first place. I remember going up one year with Lisa Thomas Management and they encouraged me to take part in a complete shite-fest of a show called *Late Night Laughs*. It was me, Matt Richardson, Angela Barnes, Ellie Taylor, Paul Sweeney and Patrick Morris. We were asked to pay a thousand pounds each for the privilege of being part of the show, and in exchange for that we played to audiences smaller than we were playing on the Free Fringe. Then we'd head to one of the artists' bars where we would see the promoters and agents all hobnobbing and having a great time, and again I'd wonder who the festival was really for.

So, I wasn't in a great mood going into my new Edinburgh show. When I was waiting backstage for the crowd to come in I was feeling a bit panicky because I didn't have what I considered to be a finished set. I went out and started limping through my act. It was going fair to middling, with me stumbling around the material, when about two-thirds of the way through a fire alarm went off. The whole building had to be evacuated. We moved out into the courtyard and I was chatting to the audience, desperate for them not to tell me what they thought of the show so far.

After about twenty minutes we went back in and I finished the show. That fire alarm meant the audience was a lot kinder to me than they might have been, so I had a better gig than I probably deserved. The next day, I was dreading the review coming out. It wasn't great. It said that my show seemed pieced together; it was bitty and wasn't as good as the show I'd done the year before. It was awful to read. And what made it worse was that I agreed with every word.

Bad reviews don't mean much when you don't agree with them. They can be painful to read, but you can at least argue with the reviewer's perspective – they didn't get the material, it wasn't for them, they're just paid to be negative. But the ones that hurt echo your own fears. The year before, a review in *Fest* magazine said: 'He may be the only comedian on this year's Fringe gunning to emulate the Child Catcher from *Chitty Chitty Bang Bang*,' and I didn't really mind because it was obvious that the reviewer, Edd McCracken, who I hope is dead now, had taken an instant dislike to me. And I wasn't quite sure what he meant. Similarly, when I was nominated for Best Newcomer in 2013, Brian Logan of the *Guardian* wrote that he agreed with all of the nominations except mine. This sounds like I scoured reviews back then – and of course I did. You work your arse off on a show, then people you don't know turn up, cast judgement on it with the stroke of a keyboard, and that can have a material effect on your livelihood. Jay Richardson's review felt like a particularly sharp kick in the balls because he'd liked my show the year before.

So that day, having read the review and bored my heavily pregnant wife shitless about it, I sat down and reworked the show from top to bottom. I worked on smoothing out the kinks. I changed the order. I turned it into more of a show. I knew there was enough in it to make a good, if not great, show: I just needed to polish it up. If this was a film, imagine a montage of me at a desk, screwing up bits of paper and putting my head in my hands, a bin in the corner slowly filling. Then, suddenly, I'm scribbling furiously. Later I close my notebook and fold my arms because I've done it! And I did.

And then I did the show and died on my arse. I couldn't believe it. I'd done worse with it than the night before. I was gutted. I had what I thought was a much improved show, and it had flopped. And now I had to deliver this piece of shit for the rest of the month. I walked out to the courtyard and saw loads of comedians I knew: James Acaster, Nish Kumar, Ed Gamble, David Trent, all really nice guys. But I saw them chatting and laughing and didn't know if I could face walking past them. Then I realized it was the only viable route out. Nish asked me how the show was going and I was honest: 'Absolute shit and I hate it here.' Nish told me he was sure I was doing great and I was just being my usual negative self. He's a nice guy.

I walked back to the flat knowing I wasn't being negative – I'd just had an absolute shocker.

I didn't change anything for the next night but I remember complaining to Seann Walsh that I had a shit show and he offered to look at it with me. He told me he thought I just needed to keep doing it and improvement would come. So I went and delivered the show exactly as before and, gradually, night after night, it began to get better and better. Don't get me wrong, there were still some nights where I insulted comedy as a genre, but it was improving.

About two weeks into the festival, Leesa gave birth to our third child. I felt she was a bit selfish about the whole thing, because she had come to the show a couple of nights before, and if she'd gone into labour during the gig she could have really done me a PR favour – not to mention giving me some great material. On the night in question, I was having an incredible evening because I was having a little drink with Sid from CBeebies. We'd taken the kids to watch his show earlier that week and I was delighted to see him at my show a couple of nights later. I had to talk to him and get a photo. Then I headed back to the flat, where Leesa said, very calmly, 'I think I'm in labour.' One of her friends was visiting at the time so she stayed with the other two, and we jumped in a cab to the hospital.

Leesa's a bit of a freak when it comes to giving birth, in that she's given birth to each of the boys within about two hours of going into labour, without any pain relief. Insanity. At least, I assume it's insanity because I have no idea how much it hurts and have honestly sometimes suspected the whole painful-labour thing is women's grand ruse and it's actually quite pleasant. If so, I have no idea how they're coordinating the operation but I'll spend the rest of my life looking for evidence.

So, Leesa gave birth to the most ferocious of our children at one a.m. on 15 August 2014, and within two hours we were in a cab home. The woman is a machine. But it also helps that by the third you literally couldn't give a shit. When we had our first, we had the car seat professionally installed. I checked it twice before I put him in and drove at 15 m.p.h. all the way home. With Charlie we hailed a taxi and threw him in the boot.

I was nominated for the Foster's Award that year, and I can tell you I didn't feel I deserved it. That's not to say I wasn't delighted – it was amazing, and it reassured me that I hadn't suddenly lost the ability to do comedy. I knew I wouldn't win, but I was delighted to be in the mix. It was the best thing that happened to me in Edinburgh. Charlie's birth was a very close second.

After that Edinburgh things really took off. I was doing more panel shows and pieces of TV, and I was asked to be the host of a Radio 4 Extra show called *Newsjack*. One of the more enjoyable and scary things I did was *Drunk History*, a show in which you get hammered, then deliver a story from history to camera. I had to have a full medical to take part, and they asked me what my favourite drink was. Then I met the production team in a bar, where they kept feeding me drink after drink until they thought I was suitably pissed to take part. And then they started filming.

I have no idea how they manage to keep you at the requisite level for long enough to film – I don't know what your drunkenness is like but mine oscillates wildly. One minute I could be talking to you about politics, the next I could be confessing that I've always been in love with you and how will we tell my wife? It's mad.

I'd been told by friends who had done the show to make sure I was really drunk because it's never as amusing when the people are just a bit tipsy. I'm a consummate professional and a total lightweight, so I got completely wasted. I used to be known among my friends for being able to handle a drink, but since I've had kids I've been known to start a fight after a lager top.

I have no recollection of how the recording went, but I do remember the producers laughing a lot. That made me feel paranoid. When you're doing recordings, producers will often laugh at what you're doing, not because they find it funny but because they want to encourage you to keep going, or give you a bit of confidence to take a joke even further. The trouble is, it can often be at your expense, particularly if you're hammered. You can definitely tell the difference between an encouragement laugh and somebody genuinely laughing. Even then, it can be a bad sign, and if the whole crew cracks up it usually means it's too much of an in-joke.

I passed out in the car on the way home, and the journey from London to Crawley lasted about a minute. I stumbled to my door, stuck my fingers up at the house where Headlight Prick lived and made my way into our front hallway. My main goal was to switch on the television, then make myself something greasy and carby to eat. I stood in front of the TV trying to get the thing turned on. I don't remember what happened next but I know that one second I was standing in the front room trying to work the remote, and the next I was kneeling on the floor with the glass coffee table in pieces behind me. The noise woke Leesa, and I believe her exact words were 'Go to bed, dickhead.' Watching the clips back was the first time I had any recollection or idea of what I had said during the recording. I was completely off my tits, shouting about Ancient Egypt.

A few months later, I was walking to a gig in Chipping Norton and headed past a pub with some young blokes sitting outside. One said, 'Romesh Ranganathan?'

I replied, 'Yes.'

'Listen, man, I just had to tell you. Saw you on *Drunk History*. You ruined it – you were way too aggressive.'

I couldn't believe it – and his mates seemed a bit taken aback. I said to him, 'I would argue very strongly that you didn't have to tell me.' If you're reading this, mate, you're a dick. I mean if you're that guy, not just if you happen to be reading this.

It was around this time that I was signed up to do *Taskmaster*. Alex Horne, who is a wonderful man, had been doing live shows where he set people tasks to perform, and they had turned the format into a TV show with a panel of five comedians competing in a series of tasks.

Once a week, we would be driven to a house in Chiswick, and would spend the day there completing various tasks. We were not supposed to communicate about how we were doing to the other contestants, and we all stuck to that, as we thought it would ruin the competitive premise of the show if we didn't. *Taskmaster* has now become a huge success but at the time we had no idea how big it would be. It just felt like a bit of a laugh.

Attempting the tasks was nerve-racking, because Alex and the crew would watch you completing these things and you'd have no idea if you were being rubbish, stupid, uninteresting or unfunny. The tasks also had an annoying quality: as soon they were finished you would immediately think of fifteen better ways to do what you'd just done. My first day was proving to be a lot of fun and the production team seemed excited that the stuff they'd planned was all working. We were coming to the end of filming when Andy Devonshire, the director, said to me, 'We've had a brilliant day. We have just one more task.'

I walked into the living room of the house and opened the task envelope. It said: 'In the lab there is a watermelon. You will have sixty seconds to eat as much of it as you can.' If you've watched the show, you'll know that I'm not the most lateral thinker, so I didn't bother tooling up. I just wandered to the door of the lab to prepare myself mentally. For some reason, I became convinced that a watermelon was really hard to open and thought I'd need to smash the shit out of it to get inside. They told me to start, and for reasons I cannot explain I ran in, picked up the watermelon and flung it to the floor. It disintegrated instantly. It was all over the bloody shop. It was an immediate reminder of how soft a watermelon is.

Undeterred, I dropped to my knees and scarfed as much of the debris as I possibly could. I was ramming it down my throat – and it was deeply unpleasant. The whistle went for sixty seconds and I tried to swallow but couldn't. My whole neck felt jam-packed with watermelon. I was struggling to breathe and started choking. My throat was blocked but I didn't feel I was in immediate danger, although I couldn't see the watermelon going anywhere. I wondered if this might just be the way I had to live from then on. My throat was making gurgling noises that I couldn't control. I sounded like a pig slowly dying.

The crew were terrified and got me to go into the toilet, where I tried to hook watermelon out of myself (hoping this wouldn't go against my score retrospectively). Eventually, there was a sudden dislodge and I went from extreme discomfort to relief and joy.

When Dave, the channel that hosts the show, saw the footage, they asked for it to be edited further as they felt it was too disturbing for public consumption.

After that episode, I did various shows that I enjoyed and that upped my profile – *Play to the Whistle, Jack Dee's Election Helpdesk*, and various panel-show guest spots. From my appearances on those shows, I've learned that I'm Marmite as a comic. The people who hate me really hate me. I can't think of the last time I did something on TV where somebody didn't send me scathing messages afterwards.

The other thing that struck me is how easily offended people are. I did a BBC3 show called *Sweat the Small Stuff*, hosted by Nick Grimshaw. It mixed comics with music stars and reality television contestants. I went into it expecting to hate everybody involved but most of the others seemed nice, friendly and genuine. For one of the challenges, Nick Grimshaw asked me to react to some childish heckles in the style of a teacher, because I used to be a teacher.

Teaching and rapping are the default things I'm asked about when I go on anything. I don't mind, but recently I said I'd rather not rap. I was on *Sunday Brunch* with Lady Leshurr who is actually good at it, so it felt a bit eggy to do a shit rap in front of her.

Anyway, one of the things Nick asked me to respond to was a heckle of 'You're shit, sir.'

I replied, 'Well, according to this register you're adopted.' Not the best joke ever, but it's off the cuff so piss off.

A few days after the show went out, I received a tweet from somebody: 'Just so you know, you're a disgusting human being and I cannot wait for you to disappear.' Now, I'm ashamed to say that I initially assumed it was actually intended for Paul Chowdhry. I was doing *Stand Up for the Week* with him at the time, and Paul, who is brilliant, loved to push the boundaries with the audience of what was acceptable. This meant people would watch the show, be offended, then look up names, see mine and assume I was him. I would then have to explain it wasn't me and redirect them to Paul's Twitter. Paul would do the same when he was mistaken for me.

So I replied, 'You may have mistaken me for someone else. How have I offended you?' He told me that he'd found what I'd said about adopted people hugely offensive: I was implying that adopted people were somehow worse than everyone else.

I had already screwed up by engaging with him, but I tried to argue my case: I explained that the joke wasn't at the expense of adopted people but about how the news was revealed to the child. He called me a fuckwit and asked me not to explain my joke to him. I ducked out of the convo, but he just carried on tweeting me, telling me he was going to use me in an adoption bullying video and informing me that he had made an official complaint to the BBC.

Much later, I did a short film for *The Premier League* show on BBC2 about referees and why on earth anybody would want to be one. After that went out, I got a tweet from someone who said their son wanted to be a referee and they had found my short extremely upsetting and had made an official complaint to the BBC.

My attitude to offence is very simple: I don't care. Obviously it's not great for the person being offended, but part of my job, as I see it, is to prod conventions, and that can sometimes upset people. If comedians worry about that too much, they lose their teeth. I respect people's right to be offended, but I reserve the right not to change in response to it. Unless, of course, I stop getting work in which case I'll change immediately – however you need me to.

10.

Mama Said Knock You Out

I got a call from Flo saying that a production company called Rumpus wanted a meeting to discuss potential projects. I had long stopped getting excited about these meetings as, although it was good to meet TV people, more often than not they led to nothing. The first time I was offered a meeting, a production company had seen me at a gig. I remember thinking this was the beginning of something huge. I phoned Leesa and told her all about it. I even started to do the embarrassing chat where you say things like 'I don't want to get carried away, but this is why you do all of the hard work, you know?' and your other half has to sit there while you pontificate as if you've cured cancer.

I turned up to the meeting brimming with excitement at what they might be asking me to host or star in. It was thirty seconds into the meeting when I realized it wasn't going to be the life-changer I'd anticipated.

'Really enjoyed your gig the other night,' said the producer opposite me.

'Thanks so much,' I replied, loath to admit to her that that was all of my best material and I had very little else to offer.

'Do you have any idea what you'd like to make?' she asked.

I didn't have a clue. I didn't know this was how it worked. I'd assumed I would walk in and Steven Spielberg or Judd Apatow or at least the head of the BBC would be there going, 'This is the guy! I've never seen anything like this talent! We need to put him on and in everything immediately!' Years later I would discover that this is how they talk to you in America but they rarely mean it. So I was supposed to have ideas. I had none.

'Well, bear us in mind when you do. We just wanted to let you know that we like you.'

The meeting was over in five minutes. I was in shock. And in Bayswater. It was awful.

The meeting with Rumpus was very different. I immediately felt more positive about it because I didn't have to go to Bayswater. I met Iain Wimbush and Emily Hudd, who had started up a small indie company and were looking to make stuff with up-and-coming talent. First of all, they really blew me away by suggesting a number of ideas they had developed featuring me. This was already going much better than the other meetings had. The truth is I had, and still have, no real idea how to make good television, so having other people come up with viable ideas was a godsend. I just decided to go by what felt like it might be good, and that's what I've done ever since. There were a few strong ideas, but I was most taken with one in particular, mainly because of the title: *Asian Provocateur*. The idea was essentially a travel show to Asia. I liked it straight away.

We had a second meeting, this time with a director called

Ben Green. Ben had just finished working with Karl Pilking-ton on his travel shows so I was amazed he had even agreed to attend the meeting. Particularly after he later informed me that we'd met before, and I'd come across as pretty arrogant. I hadn't remembered because white people all look the same to me. For all I knew it could have been Leesa.

A sitcom was being developed for Channel 4 about a choir, and I had been invited for the casting. I was extremely nervous as I had no acting experience, except for one episode of *Holby City*, in which I played a man who was getting ready for a date and decided he might have sex that night so should fix his broken bed. In the process of doing that he had, implausibly, fallen onto the floor and ended up with a screwdriver in his chest.

I remember spending my whole time at *Holby* wonder-ing how this could actually happen. If the screwdriver was lying flat on the floor, at what kind of angle would you have to approach it in order to end up with it in your chest? Conversely, what kind of fucking maniac leaves a screw-driver standing on its handle? I had no idea, but I thought it would be a laugh to be on *Holby* so I went along with it. It was a weird experience.

First, there was to be a scene where I was having sur-gery, so they needed a mould of my torso so they could make a prosthetic body. I wasn't told this in advance so I just turned up expecting to be prepped for the role when an impossibly beautiful woman came out and asked me to follow her into a dressing room to be measured up. I felt uncomfortable about this. As you know by now, I'm very self-conscious and have to build myself up to take my top off at the end of the day. I followed the woman into the room and was immediately overcome by the urge to break what I perceived to be tension, but to her the whole experience was just another task on a long list of things she had to get done that day. I was adamant that this all needed addressing, though, so when I removed my top I decided to bring an end to any awkwardness by saying, 'Sorry about my body.' She said nothing. Why would you? What I had done was extremely creepy. I was hoping to appear humorous and chilled out about the whole thing, but I came across as a needy, self-conscious pervert. What did I want from the exchange? For her to say, 'Don't apologize – I love melted chocolate'? The rest of the fitting was fairly awkward.

The acting itself represented another horror. I was put on a hospital bed and told that we were about to start filming the first scene. I had a fake screwdriver part sticking out of my chest at an angle that I felt even further undermined any semblance of realism. The scene involved me explaining my accident. Surprisingly my line wasn't 'It seems fucking impossible, doesn't it?' The director was in another room and his instructions and feedback were being radioed through. He was a very nice man, but obviously they were under time pressure and not prepared for someone with such a lack of experience on the show.

Within what felt like seconds of arriving on set I was moved into position and 'Action!' was called. I completed the scene in one take and was still buzzing when the director radioed through his instructions. These instructions were, and apologies for paraphrasing: 'Could Romesh please play the scene as if he actually does have a screwdriver in his chest – because it would probably hurt.' It turned out I had delivered the lines in the style of somebody who had a fake screwdriver stuck to his chest. I did the lines exactly the same on the second take, but with the occasional groan. They decided it wasn't going to get any better and called, 'Cut.' If you saw it, I'm sorry.

Apparently at the Channel 4 audition I had performed the lines more effectively than I did on *Holby City*, and Ben had approached me after my read-through and said, 'It was really funny, the way you said that.'

To which I had snarkily replied, 'Yes, that's what I was going for.' I don't remember it but that is exactly the sort of thing I would say. Understandably, Ben regretted saying anything. Just as I regretted being such a prick, particularly when I would have come away from that meeting thinking I'd been funny and charming. I found that terrifying. What followed was a serious period of introspection for me, when I tried to recall incidents in which I thought I'd been hilarious and engaging but in fact I might have been a weapons-grade penis.

In that second *Asian Provocateur* meeting I was yet to discover that Ben and I had met before. He did make the point, though, that for a travel show to work, it had to have a purpose. There needed to be a reason to do it, a quest. That's what separates enjoyable and engaging travelogues from the meandering ones that you tend to dip in and out of. I had just started doing a bit of material on stage about my mum's concern that I wasn't in touch enough with my culture and how she'd become worried that I was a coconut – brown on the outside, white within – so we decided that would be the impetus for the show. Mum would be the driving force behind me going to Sri Lanka to get in touch with my roots. We all felt this was a great hook for a show, and now we just had to convince the BBC and my mum (who couldn't say yes quick enough).

BBC3 gave us some money to make a 'taster' so they could see whether this would work as a series. That was a challenging proposition as they didn't give us enough money to go to Sri Lanka, so we had to make a sample in England that proved we could make a great show about travelling abroad. We decided to focus on the preparation for the trip: I was to visit a travel agent, talk to Mum about the sort of things I should do and see, have some Tamil cultural lessons to prepare me to blend in once I got there and, somewhat more randomly, I would go into a sauna fully clothed to establish how I would deal with the heat.

The first scene we filmed was the travel agent. Ben found one in Tooting and we filmed me talking to the guy about the best things to do and how to plan a trip around the island. This was all fine and generated good content for the taster, but the reason it merits inclusion here is because it led to the inception of one of my favourite elements of *Asian Provocateur*, what we referred to as the 'hip hop slow mo'.

Ben and I had been talking about music a lot and discovered we were both hip hop fans. We reminisced about growing up and visiting R&B and hip hop nights at Bagley's and Rainforest Café, and one of the observations we made was that you ended up thinking you were being really cool because of the music when you actually looked like a bit of a helmet. This gave Ben an idea. After we had finished filming at the travel agent's, he asked me to do an entrance shot into the shop, which he filmed in slow motion. He didn't tell me what he was up to, but when I came to watch the taster, he'd put 'Big Pimpin'' by Jay Z over the top. It was both badass and funny because the song was great and nostalgic but it was accompanied by a fat brown man walking into a shop to book a holiday. We knew immediately this would become a signature for the show. Well done, Ben.

The other revelation about the shooting of the taster was my mum. We had always planned to use her in the show, and I knew she was funny. What we didn't anticipate was quite how funny she would be on camera. I should add that she combined being hilarious with being almost undirectable.

Ben and Mum arranged for some of her friends to come over and we filmed a lunch scene where they would all discuss what I should do in Sri Lanka. Except my mum would come out with the most random shit. At one point she started listing places I should visit. Ben stopped filming and said to her, 'What you just said was absolutely brilliant. Can you let us get the camera set up on you and everybody quiet and say exactly that again?'

My mum said, 'Of course, darling, no problem.'

Ben set up the cameras. We got ready to roll again. 'Action!'

Mum looked across at me and said, 'Darling, you should

do more for charity. Let me tell you about one I love . . .'
She talked about it for almost two minutes.

I realized she'd gone rogue, as did Ben, but he didn't yet
know her well enough to tell her straight. So he waited for
her to finish, then said, 'That was great, Shanthi, but is it
possible to get you to say what you said before?'

My mum said, 'Of course, darling, no problem.' We roll
again. Mum says, 'There is so much vegetarian food there,
darling, but you must be careful not to get too fat. You
have a belly . . .' and then she started banging on about
that. It was amazing. It must have been frustrating for the
crew, but she was also being hilarious, so from then on
Ben would let her go off on these tangents and keep his
directing to a minimum.

I really loved that pilot tape and some of what we shot
made it into the titles of the final programme. I was excited
about doing the show, if the BBC liked the taster, of
course. One of the things we'd filmed was me having
Tamil dance lessons, and afterwards I had to give a performance to an invited audience to show what I'd learned. I
remember finding it agonizingly embarrassing and feeling
grateful I wouldn't have to go through humiliation on
that scale again. I obviously had no idea of what was soon
to come.

The BBC commissioned the show, which was to be
filmed in two parts – three weeks to shoot the first three
episodes, then a two-week break before we returned for
the second half, one episode of which was to be filmed in
India. If you've watched the show, you'll know we didn't
go to India. I say that as if it's obvious, but the number of

people who approach me and say, 'I loved your show in India,' is impressive. Almost as impressive as the number of people who tell me they really love *Travel Man* because they think I'm Richard Ayoade.

I've often tried to figure out why people do that. Obviously I don't look anything like Richard Ayoade. And many people will say to me that's racism. But is it? Someone has approached me to say they really like me, or Richard. And they've just got it wrong. I wonder if people have a set of key points they remember about people, and for me and Richard there's overlap: 'Is he deadpan? Does he travel? Is he brown? He's Richard Ayoade.' It's like a real-life game of *Guess Who?* I'd encourage everyone to add 'lazy eye' to their list of my characteristics, because at least that narrows things down.

The other day I had a woman go completely the other way. She came up to me outside a pub and asked me if I had ever been told I looked like Romesh Ranganathan. I obviously said I hadn't. She went on to tell me what programme Romesh Ranganathan had been on. In hindsight my silence was a risky strategy as she might have launched into a diatribe about how much she hated the guy, at which point I'd have had no choice but to nod along. As it was, she was fairly noncommittal.

I'm never sure of the best way to deal with people approaching me in the street, and I'm not even sure how to write about it without sounding big-headed. I will say that it's an absolute pleasure to be recognized and told that people appreciate your work, and I always feel sad that nurses and doctors who actually do important jobs don't get the same sort of recognition. And by 'I always feel sad' I mean 'That felt like the right thing to say.' The point is that 99 per cent of the time people are absolutely wonderful to talk to, but I'm hopeless at receiving compliments, so I sort of stumble my way through an interaction and get out of there as soon as possible. Otherwise, I'm pretty good at self-destructing in those moments.

I was outside a pub one night in Crawley when a girl approached me and told me she really enjoyed the show I did with Dara O Briain.

'*Mock the Week*, yeah, thanks so much,' I said.

'No,' she replied. 'The other one.'

'*Apprentice You're Fired*?'

'Nope. The one where you do tasks.'

'Oh, yeah, *Taskmaster*. Thanks. But that wasn't Dara.'

'Yes, it was.'

'It wasn't.'

'Yes, it was. Dara was in *Taskmaster*.'

'It's totally cool, I don't care, it's just he wasn't in it.'

'He was. I watched all of it.'

'Right. Well, I was in it. And he wasn't.'

'Yes, he fucking was.'

'Right, okay. Well, if you think he was, that's cool.'

'Wow. Why are you being all up yourself?'

'I'm not being up myself, it's just that Dara wasn't in *Taskmaster*.'

'Wow, okay, he wasn't in *Taskmaster*, cool. Why do you care so much?'

'I literally couldn't give less of a shit.'

It sort of went on like that. Maybe I could have handled

it better. But I came away thinking, That girl now has a story about how much of a prick I am.

Another time I was at my local with Leesa when a bloke approached me at the bar and said, 'You're that comedian, aren't you? Do us a joke, mate.'

I used my stock answer: 'I don't really do jokes, mate, I just moan.'

He looked put out. 'You're a comedian, though. Do a joke.'

'I don't really have any jokes.'

'Don't be like that. Oi, Sarah, this is that comedian you said lives in Crawley!'

Sarah comes over. 'Oh, yeah, do us a joke!'

'I don't do jokes. It was nice to meet you.'

'You're not funny in real life, are you?'

'Erm, no, I guess not.'

'Because if you were, you'd be able to just do a joke.'

'Yes, you're probably right. I'm really sorry, I'm just out for a drink. I'm going to go back to my wife.'

'Wow, I didn't think you'd be like this, mate. Just not funny.' He then declared loudly to the group of people he was with: 'I knew he'd be like that.'

About half an hour later I was headed to the toilet when I bumped into the dad of an ex-student from my teaching days. We started having a nice chat as I pretended to remember teaching his kid, when the girl of the couple from earlier came up to me with a baby in a car seat. 'This is my baby. Do a joke about him.'

'I can't really just do a joke about your baby.'

'Go on, just make one up.'

'Erm, okay, he's really ugly?'

'That's not a joke, is it?'

'Okay, sorry, I was actually on my way out.'

'That's not very nice, though, is it?'

'I really have to go, sorry.' I nearly left without Leesa. In my defence, though, the kid was hideous.

The reason we didn't go to India is because they wouldn't give us a visa to film there. Which seems weird as so many travel docs go to India, but it turned out the variable that swung it was me. They had seen my surname, assumed I was some sort of Tamil journalist, and figured I was going to do an exposé of the Indian government's role in the Sri Lankan civil conflict. What we were actually planning to do was a piece on Tamil cinema. We ended up having to relocate the shoot to Sri Lanka and it all worked out fine, depending on your opinion. You may have seen the show and decided it was appalling.

The first episode was based around my arrival in Sri Lanka and getting acclimatized. I was supposed to meet a man called Thiru – Mum claimed he was my uncle, but I never found out because he was too busy to turn up – receive a blessing and perform with a Sri Lankan rap group.

Performing with the Sri Lankan crew was the thing I was most nervous about, but it ended up being a walk in the bloody park compared to the blessing. We were in a small village in Kegalle, and the blessing was supposed to wish me well for the trip. We arrived expecting to start filming straight away, but we were informed that they still had to set up for the ceremony and we were a good few hours from it.

I have to be honest, waiting around was pretty intimidating. Nobody could give me any details of what the blessing involved, and I had never done any sort of travel show before so I definitely wasn't taking it all in my stride. People were setting up a lot of elaborate ceremonial structures, which added to quite a heady vibe. Before the ceremony started I was required to cleanse myself. It involved going to a nearby stream, stripping off and washing myself with water and lemon. This didn't make the edit, but I have since been told it might have been because they couldn't clear the Run DMC imagery on my underwear, and Ben doesn't like blurred footage. I guess what I'm saying is I washed myself with a lemon for no reason.

Because the villagers were taking such a long time to set up, Ben and Mus Mustafa, the series producer and general legend, were desperate to make use of the time. They had me wandering around talking to people and trying to get information about the ceremony. I was post-wash at this stage and barefoot in a toga. I was doing a piece to camera and reporting what I had found out about the ceremony when I felt something on my foot. I looked down: a scorpion was walking across my toes. Dear reader, I shat myself. I started screaming and hoofed the thing into the bushes. That doesn't seem like the sort of thing a vegan should do, but if I have a poisonous stinging beast on my foot, one of us is going to get fucked over.

If you want to know how the ceremony went, feel free to watch the show. I'm never going to be able to describe it and do justice to what happened, but essentially I had been mistakenly booked into an exorcism. The guys there put me into a cage, then started doing all sorts of mad stuff, like appearing possessed, rubbing chickens on my head and waving swords at me. I cannot explain to you how I felt during all of this, on what was only my second day of filming. I wondered if the whole experience would be like this bit. I also caught a sniff from a conversation between Mus and Ben that these ceremonies usually took seven hours. I was terrified, but also slightly pissed off that nobody had informed me of what an ordeal this was going to be. It was only when I looked at Ben – and you can see this on the show – and mouthed, 'What the fuck?' that I realized this was as much of a surprise to him as it was to me. What you don't see on camera is Ben throwing his arms into the air and looking genuinely panicked.

Now I know I would plead ignorance if I was a director needing a presenter to do something so ridiculous. Because what would Ben's other options be? To tell me that they needed me to sit in a cage for seven hours while people rubbed chickens on me? There's no bloody way.

It was a horrendous experience. I had no idea if any of what happened was usable or funny or interesting because I wasn't focused on any of that. I just had an incredibly traumatic night. I was shell-shocked. At least I received some great news from home that really cheered me up.

For a few years Leesa and I had been renting a house from my mum. It was the one my family had got from the council after my dad went to prison. It was also the house where I had fallen out with Headlight Prick and Leesa had wanted to kill Parking Bitch. Neighbourly feuds aside, our family had grown bigger and we were starting to feel like we needed not to be renting a house from my mum. The problem we were facing was that I was newly self-employed and we both had atrocious credit ratings. But we like a challenge, so we decided to try to buy a house.

Leesa found a place she really liked, still in Crawley, and told me how much she loved it. I really felt for her. I'd put her through hell over the previous few years, and she deserved a home she could feel happy in. I was away with work and she was trying to arrange a viewing for when I was back, but I was so desperate for her to get a place she liked I told her to put the offer in and I would see it later. She did and the offer was accepted.

Then came the issue of securing a mortgage. I spoke to a financial adviser who told me that, with the money I was making, I shouldn't have any problems borrowing the amount I required for the house. Unfortunately we did have problems – loads of problems. Every lender he tried didn't like my credit scores so we were refused time and time again. Basically, and I assume this is a trap that many people fall into, we had struggled to pay bills and keep out of overdrafts when we were on harder times and now those blips meant nobody wanted to lend us money. It was incredibly frustrating, and we wondered if it meant we would never be able to buy a property.

I kept trying different places and we kept fobbing off the vendors of the house we were buying because we didn't want them to pull out. We just couldn't get a mortgage, though, and then I had to leave for Sri Lanka to film *Asian Provocateur*. It was on the night of the blessing ceremony that I got a phone call telling me a lender was willing to put up the money. I was overjoyed, but by this stage the vendor was annoyed. He was demanding to speak to me personally, but I was abroad and filming so this was difficult. I sent him a text apologizing for dicking him about and explaining that we had sorted a mortgage and would love to continue with buying the house. He sent me a long message about how disappointed he was with my behaviour, that he felt I'd handled things badly and explained he was withdrawing from the sale. He also took it upon himself to advise me on how to deal with people in the future.

I was fairly gutted, mainly because I was going to have to tell Leesa, but also because I'd had to read this character assassination. I phoned Leesa, told her to keep looking and not get too down. Literally two days later she phoned me to say she'd found a house she loved even more than the first one. I asked her to make an offer, which she did, and again it was accepted, but this time we knew we had the mortgage in the bag. Result. And it meant that I returned from filming *Asian Provocateur* and got straight into the process of becoming a homeowner.

I imagine you may be wondering why I'm telling you a story that essentially appears to be me showing off about my good fortune. But the second reason for the inclusion of this story is the beautiful ending.

Two days before I was due to return from Sri Lanka, I received another text message from the bloke who had withdrawn from the sale. In it he asked if there was any possibility to start the sale process again because they had now decided they would like to sell to us and would even be willing to talk about bringing the price down. Well, that text message practically gave me a hard-on. I messaged him back, explaining that we were now engaged in another purchase so would not be able to buy his house. I nearly added, 'Go fuck yourself btw,' but I decided to take the higher ground of being nice in the text, then writing about the twat in a book.

Uncle Rags's inclusion in *Asian Provocateur* was a last-minute decision. He was very close to my dad and very much the maverick of the family. He dresses like a teenager, has a proper hippie vibe and is endlessly positive. We had no idea how this would come across on screen, but felt there was a good chance he would work well on the show. He was involved with episode two and the production team were keen to make sure our meeting for the first time (not first time ever, but for a while) be caught on camera – so they kept us separate after his arrival. We couldn't speak to each other until the cameras were rolling. The greeting you see on camera is the first time I had seen him since my dad passed away.

The first night Rags was filming with us, we were staying at my auntie's house. We'd just had a monster of a day, filming an emotional visit to the village where my family originated, then visiting a man who was possessed by a snake, and finally arriving at the house at about two a.m. That doesn't sound like a packed day, but what I now knew from doing *Asian Provocateur* is that filming anything takes absolutely fucking ages. The bane of our existence in Sri Lanka was tuk-tuks. They were all over the shop and loud as shit. This meant we couldn't record any sound, as they would trample over everything. Every time you see me talking to camera, that will be the fourth or fifth attempt after I'd been interrupted by tuk-tuks thrashing past.

The other issue I had was toilets. I'm squeamish about toilet use, and we were filming in some of the most rural areas of Sri Lanka so facilities were basic, to say the least. You'd need to use a toilet, ask around and somebody would say, 'Yes, of course. Just round here,' and open a gate to Hell. After I'd done that a couple of times I decided it was far simpler not to eat or drink anything and hope my body would survive off itself for a while.

We wanted to film our arrival to the house but, understandably, everyone was asleep and the house was locked up. I have to be honest, we had lost perspective at this point. We were all exhausted, and the doors being locked felt like the worst thing that had ever happened to anyone. We still had to film our arrival, though, and Ben wanted Rags to talk about his relationship with Dad. We set up the cameras, and began to film on the veranda. Rags started telling a story about how he and Dad had once got so incredibly drunk in Canada that the rest of the family were terrified and locked them up in a separate room.

There were two issues with this story. The first was that it was not funny or enlightening, but suggestive of two people with a concerning drinking problem. Second, what I just described to you in one sentence took Rags about half an hour to tell us. It's one of the few times when I've wished somebody would fall spontaneously unconscious. Of course I love my uncle and he's a goddamned legend but that was such a long story. He also told it so loudly that he woke up my auntie, who insisted on getting up and, in the style of Sri Lankan hospitality, cooking us a full dinner at two forty-five a.m. It was a long night and you can imagine how delighted I was when I watched the first edit of the episode and saw that none of that had made it in.

We had no idea if the show we were making was any good. I knew we were laughing while we made it, and it felt interesting and funny, but with comedy it's always impossible to know if you just *think* it's great and you're actually being incredibly self-indulgent. Stand-up is a lot easier in that way because it depends on immediate validation from an audience. If I write a bit, I can go to a club that night and try the stuff out. If nobody laughs I know it's awful or needs work. With filming, you're away, exhausted, dealing with a text from some prick who doesn't want to sell you his house any more, and you don't know if what you're doing is right.

Ben was also fighting our corner to keep out the more documentary-style things that Rumpus and the BBC were keen on. To be fair to them, once he'd made his position clear, I think they gave him autonomy. At least, that was what he told me, but I don't know for definite because since the whole blessing/exorcism thing I really can't trust the guy.

When we finished filming the show, we went out in Colombo for a wrap party. There was a nightclub where we became regulars, despite it being on the seedier end of the spectrum. There were loads of girls employed there to make you feel you were interesting to women. They would sit with you, laugh and find everything you were saying hilarious, and then they would ask if you wanted a drink. You would say yes and they would get the drinks for you and you would pay about ten times what you would have done had you made the five-yard walk to the bar yourself. I found these conversations pleasant until the girls said something that reminded me they were being paid to talk to me.

Sean, our soundman, seemed pretty keen to get us kicked out. He hates authority. In that particular club, every half an hour or so the dance floor would be emptied and a load of dancers would come on in saris. You were allowed to join them if you gave one of the girls a garland, which could be bought from the side of the floor. The girls would wear them and take them with them when they left. Half an hour later they would come back and you could buy the garlands again. Ingenious. Sean hated it, thought it was a con, didn't understand why we couldn't just dance and kept going onto the dance floor *sans* garland. He was repeatedly warned by the bouncers, but he hadn't finished his protest. It eventually got to the point where we were all going to be thrown out so Sean accepted that his protest dancing – which lacked any kind of discernible rhythm – was not going to bring an end to what he considered to be a deep injustice.

I remember sitting with Ben and drunkenly talking about the show we'd put together. We were very proud of what we'd done, but also aware of how difficult it was to achieve success or ratings or critical recognition for any TV show.

You can work as hard as you like, but sometimes things just go against you. Ben was more experienced than me and the last thing he said to me that night was 'Just remember, we've made a show we can be proud of. Everything else is out of our hands.'

11.

These Are the Breaks

The first night that *Asian Provocateur* went out I was on tour with Kevin Bridges. I was honoured to be supporting him because he's one of the best comedians in the world. I actually think he's underrated. I know that sounds ridiculous as he sells out arenas, but I honestly can't believe the quality of his stuff. On the tour I supported him on in 2015, he had a bit about going onto Wikipedia in the park and ending up diagnosing himself with ADHD. That might have been the best routine I've heard in the last five years. It was so good that had I gone to see him as a punter and he'd done just that five minutes, I would have felt I'd had my money's worth. In short, the boy is good.

I remember being nervous about the reaction to *Asian Provocateur*. It was different from panel-show appearances because I was fronting it, so if it was universally hated, I couldn't blame the format. I had done my twenty minutes at the top of Kev's show, and was sitting backstage when the programme went out. I looked on Twitter, and the response seemed fairly positive. What I mean by 'fairly positive' is that about 75 per cent of people were saying, 'Enjoying this,' or whatever and only 25 per cent were saying things like 'This is a piece of shit and I hope him and his family die', which was a result. Although I remember being a little bit worried because a couple of people took deep offence to the way I described that blessing/exorcism thing and started telling me how disrespectful I'd been. One person even tried to set up an online petition. On the whole, though, I felt fairly satisfied with the response. Except for all the upsetting tweets about how funny my mum is.

It was only a few weeks later that I had any inkling of how the show had changed my profile. I was due to do *Live at the Apollo* part of the way through Kev's tour, which meant I had to get together a brand new twenty minutes of material. I didn't want to be trying out new stuff at Kev's gigs because supporting someone of his stature is difficult enough without running out your new crap. So what I would often do was book a gig down the road from the tour show. This was particularly weird in Glasgow, because I was supporting Kev at the Hydro, a 16,000-seater venue, then went down the road to the Yes Bar, which seated about thirty people, to try out my stuff for the Apollo.

One night I was supporting Kev in Manchester and had been booked to go and do ten minutes at the Comedy Store afterwards. I did the Kev spot, then headed down to the Store.

The compère, Rob Rouse, who is absolutely phenomenal, introduced me as a surprise guest and I came onstage to what was probably the loudest reception I had ever had. My ears weren't used to hearing such cheers, because when I was announced to come on at the top of Kev's show, I could usually hear a member of the audience go, 'Oh, for fuck's sake.' Anyway, I walked on and they were cheering and shouting. I waited for them to settle, but they didn't. I started going into the material I was trying out and they would just shout quotes from the show at me. It was insane. I was completely blown away by it. It was also the first night someone shouted, 'Where's your mum?' which I found funny then. Little did I know how much of a soul-crushing chant that would become.

I also started to notice the difference when I was out and about. I was getting recognized more, and people were approaching me to tell me they enjoyed the show. I also got lots of people saying, 'I used to hate you, but I'm enjoying your show,' which is a weird bit of feedback to process. I even started to notice that the receptions at the Kev gigs were getting warmer. It definitely felt like a big step up.

A few months later, I found out I'd been nominated for a BAFTA for best entertainment performance. I could not believe it. It genuinely had never entered my mind that I could ever even be in the reckoning for a bloody BAFTA. On those occasions they're pretty careful about who gets tickets to the awards ceremony: I was given a plus one. I really wanted Leesa to come, as she had been through so much for the sake of my career. I also wanted my mum to come, because she had been in the show and she bloody loves celebrity stuff. But extra tickets are five hundred pounds! If you ever have to choose between your wife, your mum or spending a fortune, just pay the money. It's the easy way out. I took them both because I knew I'd never get nominated again, so thought we should make an evening of it.

The BAFTAs were so mad. I also got an indication of how much of a bottom feeder I was, when walking the red carpet and constantly being asked if I could move so someone could get photos of people who were actually famous. I don't mind stuff like that, not because I'm such a cool chilled-out guy, but because in truth I was too busy losing my shit at the people we were seeing around us.

The one person I was really blown away by was Lenny Henry – I'd grown up watching him. The guy is a legend. I used to sit with my family and watch every single thing he did. I worshipped him. I even bought his graphic novel *The Quest for the Big Woof*, which I bloody loved too. And I've always admired all of the work he has done to encourage more diversity in the arts and television, which is something I hope to do too, but maybe not right now because I don't really want ethnic-minority comedians eroding my USP.

I was walking through the foyer to the awards and as I strolled past him he called me over. Lenny Henry called me over! He told me he'd watched and enjoyed *Asian Provocateur* and that he loved my mum. Wonderful. I think I was too star-struck to say much in response.

Two years later, in 2017, I ended up working with Lenny as I was asked to be involved with Comic Relief. Of course I said yes. Partly because I wanted to help people in less fortunate circumstances, but mainly because the show was a big deal.

That particular Comic Relief was somewhat controversial. They had chosen to film it all in a studio set to look like a bar, which gave it a kind of *TFI Friday* feel, but also meant that the sound was a nightmare. They were jumping from place to place and there were loads of technical issues. At one point Miranda Hart, having rehearsed a bit to camera where she's walking with a trolley, got to the actual set and had no autocue so ended up freestyling her bit without anyone noticing. It felt pretty chaotic, which was what they were going for, but it got slaughtered in the press. They also said that less money had been donated as a result. I don't mind being called shit in the papers. What I do mind is being accused of being so shit that children in Africa are losing money.

I should clarify that this was all in my head. I smoked a lot of marijuana when I was younger and I'm convinced this has left me with a deep-seated lifelong paranoia. I once thought I'd upset a colleague at work so I texted her to apologize. When she didn't reply I asked her just to acknowledge receipt of the text even if she didn't forgive me. Then I asked her to please tell me what to do to make it up to her. Then I sent her a text apologizing again and explaining I wouldn't make things awkward at school by talking to her and could we just draw a line under it? I received a text later saying: 'Phone was off because I was in the cinema. Are you fucking mad? I have no idea what you're talking about.'

On the way to the awards, Leesa, Mum and I got a car together and all those two shitheads would talk about was how much they wanted to see Idris Elba. My mum was determined to meet him. I'm not sure she's watched anything with him in it, I think she just wants to jump his bones, which is so disgusting a thought that my fingers are literally curling as I write. Leesa loves his work, but also wants to jump his bones, which sets up the prospect of one of the most upsetting threesomes of all time.

We sat and watched the awards, and I was asked to present one with Katherine Ryan, just before it was time for my category to come up. We presented our award then went off with the winners (*Have I Got News for You*). As I wandered backstage, a couple of people said, 'Well done!' and looked at me as if I'd just won something. And then something horrible happened. I became convinced that I was about to win and they already knew. It was absurd. You know when you're waiting for a result for something, like exams or a job interview or a medical test, and you always look for a sign that predicts what the outcome might be? Do you do that? Or am I just a mad bastard?

I went back and took my seat, and knew that my award was coming up shortly because a camera positioned itself right by my face. I had a plan that I was going to do a *faux*-angry thing into the camera when I lost. It was going to be hilarious. Unfortunately, however, I'd managed to convince myself through the mystic signs backstage that I might have won, so when Keith Lemon was announced as the winner I was actually disappointed.

They do a big dinner after the awards, and as we all headed downstairs to eat, Leesa nipped into the smoking area. I was smoking properly at the time, but now I've gone part-time. Which basically means I don't touch a cigarette for a year or so, then I chain smoke for two months and then I give up again and so on. I've recently decided this is unacceptable, so have sworn off cigarettes completely unless someone offers me one or I've been drinking or I feel like having a cigarette. This whole 'not really smoking' thing gave me a surprise recently when a mate offered me a cig and I was struck by how bleak the packaging has become. I know they've had warnings on cigarette packets for a while, but I cannot believe any of us are still smoking with what they have on them now: the packet I took one from had a message on the top saying something like 'You should probably call your friends and family right now because you're about to die, you disgusting piece of shit. Your body will then be placed in a bin.' I was shocked, but I took one because I have zero willpower.

I stepped outside with Leesa and we bumped into Idris and Tom Hiddleston. Idris said hello to me. We'd met before at a gig in Soho. I was doing a set and he was in the audience, and we had a drink afterwards: he chatted to me about comedy and Arsenal. I remember this well, because Flo was with me and had lost her shit because she's a massive fan and wants to jump his bones too. I think it might be a prerequisite that every woman in my life wants to shag Idris Elba. I said hello to Idris and Tom, and started to have a little chat. I was a bit out of my depth so ended up doing a little bit of sub-par banter – or that's how Leesa described it to me afterwards. It was then that Tom whispered something in Idris's ear and they moved away. Now, I have no idea what was said. It might have been 'Shall we try to talk to some people over here just yards away from Romesh and Leesa?' I don't know. What I do know is it immediately followed my shit banter. I had mugged myself off.

We went back into the venue and I sat down for dinner with the others. Mum immediately said to me, 'I just saw Idris. Can you introduce me?'

I had to say, 'Look, Mum, I know you really want to meet him, but I'm afraid I can't introduce you because I've used up all of my awkward for one night.' After that embarrassing end to the chat, there was no way I was taking her over to meet him. I didn't fancy ending the evening with a restraining order. Mum immediately looked pissed off and stopped talking to me.

Throughout the night we met loads of cool people – Reggie Yates, James Nesbitt, Krishnan Guru Murthy, the People Just do Nothing boys, and we talked to all of them but not to each other. At the end of the night I was sitting with Mum and asked her if she'd had a nice evening.

'No.'

'Why not?'

'You didn't introduce me to Idris Elba so I hated it.'

At this point, I was annoyed. I generally don't get annoyed with my mum. She went through hell for us and I'll never take that for granted, but now she was out of order. I said to her, 'You know I had to pay a lot of money for your ticket?'

'You shouldn't have bloody bothered.'

Well, that was it. We stopped talking to each other. When Flo and Leesa rejoined us, they must have wondered what the hell was going on as it had got practically Arctic in their absence. They kept asking us if everything was okay and I kept saying we were fine because I felt that would be less awkward than shouting, 'This woman is an ungrateful cow!'

We sat in silence for the whole journey back. I was actually furious because, instead of having a nice evening, I had not won a BAFTA and my mum had stopped talking to me. We pulled up at Mum's house, didn't say goodbye, and as she got out, the driver said, 'Did you get to meet Idris Elba, then?' I didn't tip the prick.

Ben and I had always said we would do only one series of *Asian Provocateur* because the premise was so neat, and we'd done everything we wanted to do with it. We couldn't return to Sri Lanka because we'd be looking for stuff to do and the whole thing would feel too staged. So, we were ready to go off and work on something else, but then Rumpus said there would be an appetite for a second series. We really weren't sure at first, but then we decided that if we were going to do it, we'd need to make a completely different show and really take some risks. It would still be a travel show, but we wouldn't go to Sri Lanka or somewhere similar: we had to find a new purpose. We knew some people might not go for it, but we felt it was creatively the much more interesting thing to do, rather than churning out more of the same.

We were looking for a reason to go somewhere, which was when I pointed out how much family I had in North America. This felt like a good starting point, because it served the remit of being completely different from the first series and was also the natural progression: I'd returned to my roots, now let's see where the different parts of family had ended up. And, of course, Mum would be joining us.

That America shoot was a nightmare from start to finish. First, it went massively over budget because the Brexit issue shifted the dollar exchange rate and made the show loads more expensive. Then we had some of the worst fixers in history. Fixers are local agents who help you organize and sort stuff out for the show, arranging permits, helping with logistics and whatever else you need to make things go smoothly. When we were in Florida we had Steve and Debbie. Steve was incredible: he would combine looking exceedingly efficient with being totally incompetent. So Mus would have conversations with him like this: 'Do you know the area we're filming in tomorrow?'

'Yessir, I do.'

'So do you think it would be possible to sort out a place for us to have lunch after we film the wrestling?'

'Yessir, no problem.'

'Okay, so we'll be having lunch at two. Is that cool?'

'Yessir, absolutely.'

The next day Mus would say, 'Right, cool, did you sort a lunch location?'

'No, sir, I did not.'

'Any reason?'

'I just could not do it, sir.' That was pretty much what he did with every request.

The best moment we had was when my uncle Guru was supposed to be taking us across the Deep South in an RV. They had found him an absolute shit-heap of a vehicle to drive us around in. We filmed him arriving in it, and then we had to move to the lunch location that Steve had not secured. Most of us got a ride in the crew vehicles, while Steve drove the RV to meet us at the restaurant. Halfway there we got a call from him telling us it had broken down. Not a massive surprise as it was rank. He got a ride with Debbie and met us for lunch.

Later that day, Mus sent Steve to get the RV picked up. We needed to fix it so we could carry on with the journey. The only problem was that Steve couldn't find it. He was gone for ages before he phoned Mus and Ben to inform them it had been stolen. This raised a couple of questions: (a) Why the hell would anyone want to steal a piece of crap like that? and (b) How the hell did they steal a piece of crap like that? It wasn't running! Suffice to say, after we returned to the UK, we received an email informing us that Steve had realized he'd been looking in the wrong place and the vehicle had been found.

Another time during that trip, we were in some woods and I was doing a piece to camera for the end of one episode. As I was talking I felt a small pinch on my collarbone. I didn't think anything of it. We wrapped, then got into the van to head to Atlanta for a meal and a few drinks to celebrate the end of the first half of the series. On the way, I started to feel itchy. All of a sudden, Sam, the camera-man, looked at me and went, 'Bloody hell, mate, are you okay?' He showed me a picture and my whole face and body were inflamed with hives. I looked appalling and my skin was on fire. Ben insists to this day that I was being a baby but it was horrific. What made it worse was that Mum and my brother Dinesh had come out for the episode but were in a different vehicle. When we all got out they looked at me and freaked out. Mum was going, 'Oh my God, my darling, what happened to your face?'

I didn't fancy going out in public looking like the Case Zero in *28 Days Later* so they went for the meal while I took an antihistamine and went to sleep. When I woke up a few hours later the hives were gone and I was bang up for going out to join them. They were all headed to Atlanta's oldest strip club, Clermont Lounge, which turned out to be less a strip club than a bar. The DJ was playing funk and hip hop and the strippers were all fifty-plus and I think doing it ironically, unless it was a fetish thing. The funniest thing about the whole affair was the look on the face of Uncle Guru, who was bitterly disappointed.

In our early twenties, my brother and I had gone to visit our cousins and uncles in Toronto. Once the youngsters had gone to bed, our uncles said, 'Right. We've been waiting to have a night out like this with you. Let's go to a strip club!' They took us to a place called Tony's. Neither of us had ever been to anything like it before. I have been to many since, for stag dos and the like, and I think it's fair to say they're awful. It's so awkward, and the men all look like perverts. A girl comes over to talk to you and you sit there nervously waiting for them to ask if you want a private dance. It's at this point you get the impression that the strip club you're in is run by the Mafia, so you can either get your head kicked in or pay for a dance and sit around awkwardly, not knowing where to look.

To make my position clear, I hate strip clubs at the best of times. They are seedy and brimming with weirdos, and not once have I thought having a horny uncle in beside me would improve the experience.

We took a seat and one uncle* took on a weird Sri Lankan Tony Soprano vibe. He looked around the club and said, 'Pick any girl and I'll get you a dance.' I didn't feel comfortable so I didn't say anything. Then he said again, 'Pick someone. It's on us!' I realized I would have to pick a girl so I just pointed at one who was walking past. My uncle called her over: 'Look after this young man. He's like a son to me.'

The girl took me to a booth, saying all sorts of embarrassing untrue things, like 'You're so hot. I'm going to enjoy this.' I know this is all supposed to make it hotter and less seedy, but it really does break the spell when somebody tells you something patently untrue. I sat down and she said, 'Just so you know it's twenty dollars a dance.'

I said, 'All good. My uncle's paying.'

What followed was a period of her gyrating and whispering more lies in my ear, gyrating and whispering and gyrating. I spent the whole time feeling intermittently awkward and aroused. Every now and again she would say, 'Your uncle's got this, right?' and I would just nod. This seemed to go on for ages until eventually she said, 'Are you sure your uncle's got this?'

I was a bit confused. 'Yes,' I said. 'Why?'

'Because right now you're on three hundred dollars.'

It was only then that I realized I was an idiot. I was sitting there expecting her to go, 'Okay, that's you done,' but

* Uncles have been anonymized to avoid family issues, but they're proper pervs.

I was being charged per song. What kind of fucking system was that? I've never heard of anything in the service industry where the staff keep going until you say stop. All of these thoughts went through my head, but they didn't change the fact that I was three hundred dollars in the hole. I jumped up and said, 'Oh, shit! Sorry, I've never been to a place like this before. I didn't know how it worked.' Now, to be fair to the girl, that wasn't her problem. She had checked with me numerous times that I was able to pay and I had said yes. How was she to know that I was the type of moron to think that twenty dollars gets you an hour-long lapdance?

She said, 'Look, don't worry, I'll give you fifty dollars off.'

That was really nice of her, but my panic meant I showed her virtually no gratitude. I was wondering desperately how to get out of this because I didn't want to sit back with my uncles and tell them they had to pay the woman hundreds of bucks because I'm a fucking idiot. I started looking at the doors to see if I could make a run for it and meet my uncles and brother later, but that looked unlikely. In any case, it's more difficult to run quickly with an erection.

I ended up paying the girl everything in my wallet, which was about a hundred dollars, and she honoured the discount. When I went back and my uncles started ribbing me about how long I'd been, she asked them for 150 and they suddenly thought I was the man for getting such a long dance for so little money. I had come out of the whole thing looking like a legend. That made it even funnier when I saw the abject despair on Uncle Guru's face when we went into the Clermont Lounge. Not that it was him that took us to the strip club. Not at all.

That was my favourite part of the series, possibly because my brother came out for it. The one regret I have about getting family involved in my TV projects is that I haven't included him in more stuff. He's very similar to me, albeit younger, funnier and better-looking, but the similarity means he's less suited to being in the shows: you're looking for points of difference and friction, and while my brother and I do bicker it's not quite the same. Having said all of that, he probably gave us the best episode of them all.

At one point, we went to take part in some wrestling training, and it quickly became apparent that Dinesh was a brown Hulk Hogan. He was incredible. I, on the other hand, found it really hard and the wrestling coach found me disrespectful and was shouting at me, which was funny but took me back to the days of being the fat kid in PE. Dinesh came outside to console me (he took the piss out of me later for being a punk) and it was one of the most emotional bits of the show. He's started doing stand-up now so I hope soon we can do something together at some point.

We've always shared a dark sense of humour. The day after Dad died when I went round to visit Mum, Dinesh and his wife Claire were already there. I started talking, then Dinesh said, 'I don't care what you do, mate, as long as you don't make the horrific noise you made when you found out Dad was dead.' What then followed was thirty seconds of him mocking the sounds I'd made when I cried the night before. Harsh, but exactly what the situation needed.

There has been talk of a third *Asian Provocateur* season, but I can't see it happening any time in the near future. We were dead set on not doing any more until Rumpus asked us if we might reconsider, at which point we discussed a few ideas. We originally talked about doing Australia, then settled on going to India, which would now almost definitely let us in as we had previous series to show that it was less about incisive journalism than it was about a fat idiot stumbling around a foreign country. It was to be a trip with me, Mum, Dinesh and Uncle Rags making our way across the subcontinent together, which was the trip that Rumpus had originally envisaged in our initial meeting.

Ben had always been against doing another series. He thought we had pushed our luck with series 2 and were lucky that came out well, and that the whole concept was done. I tended to agree with him. Rumpus were keen for us to explore it, though, so they accepted some money from the BBC to develop the idea. Ben and I sat down and thrashed out what a trip to India might look like, and we'd made a bit of progress before he went off to America to film a little-known series called *Carpool Karaoke*.

Rumpus and I continued developing the third series, but at the same time an opportunity in America had suddenly emerged. One of the executives on *Carpool Karaoke* had watched *Asian Provocateur* when researching Ben and loved it. He wanted a show like it for America. Ben and I had been talking about other projects and had come up with the idea of me doing something in the States, where at least part of the story would stem from my attempting to build a profile over there. We pitched this idea to the executive and he loved it. They went off to sell it and it was bought by Showtime. Amazing news. However, this presented a complication. Completing the Showtime show meant that we would not be able to do series three of *Asian Provocateur*. We weighed all of this up, and decided that we would rather try something new than go back to something we had already done. I can't see us ever doing another *Asian Provocateur*, but give it six months of the phone not ringing with work, and I'll book the flights myself.

12.

This Is America

I've always loved American stand-up. Richard Pryor is my all-time favourite – I even have his face tattooed on my arm – but the first US comedian I watched and loved was Eddie Murphy. I hadn't discovered him through stand-up: I'd watched *Beverly Hills Cop* and kind of fallen in love with him. We used to do a weekly video-shop visit and each pick a film to watch. The whole family was into comedy. Mum loved and still does love the slapstick stuff.

She's a huge Peter Sellers fan, so we watched a lot of Inspector Clouseau. Based on her consumption of comedy she must have amnesia, because she's watched all of those films dozens of times with absolutely no diminishing returns to her enjoyment. It's actually anger-inducing: I wish I enjoyed anything as much as she enjoys seeing Inspector Clouseau being bitten for the fortieth time. She actually laughed more with subsequent viewings: she would get us to rewind the tape, then laugh at the anticipation of the moment coming and piss herself silly when it happened. She's not the biggest stand-up fan, though. She comes to watch as many of my gigs as she can, but her understanding of what is good and what is not when it comes to my comedy is non-existent. It's actually quite sweet. She once came to a work-in-progress gig where I died on my arse, and as I walked out afterwards, she came up and hugged me and told me how proud she was. If I didn't know her, I'd have thought she was taking the piss.

She was with a couple of friends that night and they really got on my nerves. That gig was one of my first try-outs of what eventually became *Irrational*, my last tour. I had just put together a load of ideas and was testing them for the first time. Every time I write a show I have one goal: to make it better than the last. Which means that I'm trying something different in each show to mix it up. At least, that's what I think I'm doing, although I'm sure you're probably just seeing varied combinations of 'I'm brown, I'm brown, I have kids, I'm brown, I have kids, I have kids, I'm brown and I'm fat.'

On that particular night I'd tried some stuff about being brown and fat and it had failed. I was gutted, but the whole point of those gigs is to see what lands and what doesn't, so I didn't dwell on it. Then I came out to see my mum, and one of her friends, who wasn't biologically hardwired to love everything I do, said, 'I preferred the stuff you did before, to be honest.' I was raging, but obviously I thanked her for her feedback.

So, my love for stand-up began when I watched Eddie Murphy's *Raw* and thought it was the most amazing thing I'd ever seen. It was unbelievable. He just had a microphone and was making people lose their shit. There's a bit where he does an impression of Richard Pryor that made me go and check out Pryor's stand-up because I found it so funny. Have you watched any Eddie Murphy recently? It's still amazing if you're a fan of homophobia.

I'm constantly accused of being obsessed with American stand-up. I did a feature with Kevin Bridges and Frank Skinner a while back where we had to name our favourite comedians of all time. Frank couldn't believe how many of mine were American. Obviously there are plenty of incredible British comics too, Frank being one. I love Stewart Lee, and I think Kev, Jon Richardson and Michael McIntyre are amazing. But my love of American stand-up meant I'd always wanted to see how I'd get on in America as a comedian. So the Showtime series seemed an amazing opportunity.

Making TV in America is totally different, though, and you do have to tune out a lot of the things you're told by some Hollywood types. I remember being told by an American agent that he was amazed I wrote my own stand-up, which is obviously what almost every single stand-up comedian does, bar Rob Beckett, who just steals my jokes and replaces 'fat' or 'Asian' with 'teeth'.

My first gig in America did not bode well for the future. It was while I was filming a documentary about Richard Pryor and I went to the Laugh Factory on Sunset Boulevard to do a set. The compère was a cool black guy, and he almost had a physical reaction to my name. 'I can't fucking say that, man,' was his response when I told him my surname. 'I'm just going to say Romesh.'

I went up and did my bit. Because we were filming it as part of the Pryor doc, I had to reveal my tattoo and talk about it. I wrapped the set, which had gone fine, then the guy went back up and said, 'Why does an Indian man have Richard Pryor on his arm? Imma get Mahatma Gandhi,' which was his attempt at an Indian comedian reference, I guess. He then went, 'How famous does that man think he is? Just going by one name? Imma just be Romesh.' I really hope that guy's dead now.

Marijuana is legal in LA, which means you have these shops where you can buy weed, but also anything you can imagine to do with it. You can get cookies, cakes, vapes, Gummy Bears. They even put THC in crisps, which I think is madness. Imagine putting THC in the thing you crave when you get the munchies.

I had mentioned how amazing I thought this was to the crew on the doc, and on the last night Kev, the main cameraman, told me he'd got me a present and pulled out a marijuana vape. I was unreasonably excited. My agent, Flo, and Chris Cottam, the director – I went on to work with him on *Misadventures* – sat down to have a couple of beers and I chatted to them, but was mainly thinking about getting back to my room so I could have a go on the vape. Later I discovered it's so lax over there that I could have had it then and there in the outdoor drinking area. After we finished our drinks I went upstairs, put on *Curb Your Enthusiasm* and turned on the vape (which sounds nowhere near as cool as 'lighting up'). It was extremely smooth, but I didn't feel I was getting anything from it. So I had a bit more, then a bit more, and finally I properly smashed it.

What followed was a night of hell. I was absolutely off my tits. The room was spinning and I couldn't focus on Larry David on the TV. I had overmedicated in the extreme. Being in a hotel room somehow made it worse. I was now desperate to undo what I had done because I didn't think I'd make it through the night feeling that awful. I wanted to be sick, but had lost the ability to *be* sick, and the room suddenly felt like the most hostile environment I had ever been in. I grabbed the room-service menu, and ordered every vegan item on it. I then sat on the edge of my bed and waited, trying not to cry. When the food arrived, I was dismayed to find that the door to my room was a five- to six-mile walk from my bed. I had zero idea how I was going to get there, so I just pleaded with the man to let himself in, which he did, placing the food on the table before somehow getting me to sign for it. That was a harsh lesson. Vaping is terrible.

One of the most frequently asked questions off the back of the *Misadventures* series is whether I was stoned when I left the Rasta museum. Ethiopia is the spiritual home of Rastafarianism, and as part of my trip there, we were shown round a museum made and lived in by a man called Ras La Mumba, who gave us the tour while smoking a spliff the size of a toddler's leg. After the show went out, I got loads of tweets and messages asking me if I'd got high with Ras. The man was on another planet, and we all got high just looking at him.

Anyway, I occasionally think about dabbling a bit when in the UK. However, marijuana is completely illegal in the UK so I would never partake in it. I have however, written this short story about what might happen if I had decided to buy weed in the UK. Which I wouldn't. Here it is.

I phoned up a mate and asked him if he knew where I could get weed because the last time I'd bought marijuana people still thought minidiscs were the future. About three hours later a BMW pulled up to the house with a bag of weed and a set of drug-dealer stereotypes. I walked over to the car and the guy told me off for approaching the window and asked me to get into the back. I was tempted to reassure him that we were in Crawley and not, as he seemed to believe, an episode of *The Wire*. I took the weed and the telling-off and returned to the house, where I found a nice little Tupperware container to put it in. I sealed it all up and put it into a drawer in the dining room.

About an hour later I was watching TV when Leesa came in. 'Have you been buying marijuana?'

'Why do you ask?' I replied, wondering if the drug-dealer had been correct and we'd been made or something.

'Well, it's just that the dining room smells like Bob Marley's Hoover bag.'

I went downstairs, trying to ignore how old-fashioned Leesa's metaphor was, but I was immediately distracted by the potent smell. She was right. It absolutely reeked. It actually smelt like the perfect place to send the kids on a time-out. They'd come back completely calm and wanting some Doritos. I later discovered the best thing to do with weed is to put it into a container, then stick it in the freezer, but I really probably shouldn't be giving marijuana storage tips in a book.

THE END.

Starting to put the show together felt crazy. Before we began filming, Ben and I had to go out to LA to start prepping the show and work out exactly what it would be.

And we were doing that at CBS studios in Los Angeles, which was a headfuck. It's properly showbiz, and we were based in an office a floor above where James Corden makes *The Late Late Show*. I popped in to see him and it was surreal seeing a British man I knew from doing *A League of Their Own* in that swanky office set-up, with CBS executives milling around. Later on I went to watch him taping *The Late Late Show* and it was really weird to see it all. I think that was the main thing I had to get over in LA. The fact I was in and among showbiz. That and the insanity-inducing jetlag.

I'm shit with jetlag. In 2017 I did a month in Australia and New Zealand. The flight to Australia was a real ordeal. I'm one of those people who gets incredibly emotional at altitude, plus this time I was upset to be away from home for so long, plus I got drunk and watched *Lion*, a film based on a true story about an Indian boy who gets separated from his family, never finds them, and ends up being adopted in Australia. Then he eats some Indian food and decides he wants to find his mum. It's a breathtakingly mixed bag of a film, because the first half is an amazing child actor portraying the terror of being separated from his family in India, and the second half is mostly a man using Google Earth. Anyway, the kid in the first section of the film is an incredible actor, and reminded me a lot of our youngest son, so I found that section hugely emotional. And I was drunk because someone had bought me a ticket in business class.

Business class is unbelievable. I've never paid for it myself, but I'm occasionally lucky enough to fly in it for, well, business – for shoots or tours or whatever. It's so sick, or at least it would be if it wasn't for the fact that most of the time if I'm in business class the film crew still have to fly economy. You sit together at the airport, but when you board the plane, you turn left and sit up front in luxury, while they're stuck at the back next to the toilets. It's so awful. For them. For me it's fucking awesome. No, the truth is that I find the whole thing a bit awkward. What I try to do now is avoid eye contact with them as I board the plane.

I spent just over a week in Melbourne, then headed to Sydney and finally Auckland. I was away for four weeks and I spent the whole trip on British time. This wasn't deliberate. I'm just awful at adjusting. It was embarrassing. I would spend whole days in my hotel room, going between sleeping, eating and Netflix. I was sharing a venue with Phil Jupitus, whom I saw every day after his show. He would tell me he'd been visiting art galleries, checking out the scenery and landscapes, soaking up the culture. He'd then ask what I'd been up to and I'd have to tell him I'd slept until an hour before I had to leave for my show, eaten something left on my room-service tray from breakfast, then turned up at the gig. It was disgusting and awful and I'm sure Phil thinks I'm a dreadful human. But I can at least say one thing for Australia: their hotels are lovely.

So we're at CBS and have established the idea for the show: I will move with my family to America, then try to break it. We decided it would be nice to have a tangible target, so I booked out the Greek Theatre. How well we filled it would be the measure of how much of a profile I'd been able to generate in the months running up to the gig, and we'd just go with whatever happened as our big ending. Of course my family would be in the show too, which, in the case of Mum and Uncle Rags, was not a problem: both of them are seasoned showbiz veterans.

The big issue was Leesa. She had and has absolutely zero interest in being on television, or being recognized, or anything to do with celebrity. When I get recognized and/or asked for photos, her ability to disappear is unparalleled. So I had to convince her to be involved by telling her that (a) she wouldn't be on screen a lot, and (b) it was for Showtime so they wouldn't be showing it in the UK. Both of those things proved to be untrue. We would also be living in Los Angeles with my mum in the house and my uncle in the garage. I was jeopardizing my marriage for my career.

I hired a Chevrolet Suburban for Leesa and me to travel around LA and the thing was like a tank. It was easily the biggest car I'd ever driven, and I've never seen a car that big in the UK. It was ridiculous. The second night after Leesa and the kids arrived in LA I was trying to impress them by taking them around Beverly Hills and showing them the sights, while explaining to Leesa that she was going to be in the show a little bit longer than I had initially intimated. A typical Romesh evening unfolded: I got us stuck in traffic for two hours straight, Leesa was pissed off and the kids were losing their shit, finding some more shit, then losing that. We were driving along Sunset Boulevard, and I spotted a McDonald's Drive Thru. Suddenly I had a way to appease the children. Chicken nuggets.

A lot of people ask me if I've brought up my kids as vegans and the answer is no. And I know this offends vegans. In fact I mentioned getting the kids McDonald's on Adam Buxton's podcast once, then saw some vegan comment that it was disgusting and I'd really let the community down. Let me say this: I don't want to be part of the 'community'. I decided to be vegan because I'm opposed to animals being harmed for my consumption, and that's it. I also understand that the ideal for vegans is that everybody becomes vegan because then you know that animals are not being harmed. I get all of that. But I'm not interested in 'converting' people unless they ask to talk about it. And then it's possible I can't be arsed.

The boys were absolutely buzzing about going into McDonald's, so I drove in, mainly in the hope that this would calm them down. If it failed, I was seriously considering getting them some weed vapes. The drive thru had a tunnel you had to go through, and I swear to God it was designed to be like a task from the bloody *Crystal Maze*. I couldn't navigate it. First, I was driving a car the size of a military attack vehicle, and second, the tunnel got narrower and narrower, like we were going into Willy Wonka's Chocolate Factory. I pulled up to the counter, where the woman, who had been trained to take orders inaccurately and show zero emotion on her face, recorded an order for three Chicken McNugget meals and a Diet Coke as 'a bag full of random shit we found out back'. I thanked her and went to drive off, but the car was almost too long to make the turn inside the tunnel. So what actually happened was I thanked her, then drove forward to the sound of screeching metal against concrete and absolutely no reaction from the woman. I can only assume that happens to every customer as I don't think she even blinked. I then reversed, adjusted my position and drove forward, repeating the screeching metal on a different panel of the car. We picked up our incorrect order and headed off, formulating a plan between us to return one day and burn that McDonald's to the ground.

Probably the most insane thing about the whole America experience was the proximity to celebrity. The truth is, once the novelty of being in LA wore off, you were doing a job like any other. It was meeting people that was mad. And I'm not typically one for being star-struck unless it's Lenny Henry. And, occasionally, a rapper or a footballer I'm obsessed with.

I was supporting Kevin Bridges in Manchester and we were there for a couple of nights. I'd been to do that gig at the Comedy Store, and then we'd gone out and got really drunk. I remember sitting in the hotel bar at three a.m. and we were discussing absinthe. Kev decided we should try some. I guess what I'm trying to say is we were proper lads doing what lads do. Legends.

The next day we were off to watch the Manchester derby and I met Kev in the same bar in which we had been such completely hilarious legends, and not shouty wankers in any way. We were both struggling badly so were smashing coffee in a desperate hope of feeling better. We were just planning to leave when Kev said, 'Rom, that's Ian Wright over there.' And it was Ian Wright, Arsenal's second highest goal scorer of all time and just general hero. One of my favourite Ian Wright moments was when they thought he

was about to break the record at Arsenal: Nike printed him
a T-shirt to wear under his kit that said '178 – Just Done It',
which is probably as charming as brand placement gets.
Then Wrighty revealed it a goal too early. You had to be
there, really. Which I wasn't. To give you an idea of my
admiration for the man I have one of his signed, framed
Arsenal shirts taking pride of place in a temporary storage
spot until Leesa allows me to put it up.

Kev knew how much I love him and told me to go and
say hello but, as mad as it sounds, I didn't want to. This
wasn't the way I wanted to meet Ian Wright. I wanted to be
completely charming so that Ian Wright would think I was
an amazing dude he wanted to be best friends with. No
good could come from meeting him now. I explained this
to Kev and he understood because he too was craving the
sweet embrace of death. We got up and began to make our
way out, when suddenly Ian spoke to us: 'Kevin Bridges!
Hello, mate.' Kevin, you recognizable wanker! Now we
had to go over and I was going to have to stand next to Kev
like a tag-along.

We walked over and Kev said hello, then introduced
me. 'Oh, yeah, I know you! You've been doing that show
in Sri Lanka with your mum. I love that show.'

I nearly died. I couldn't believe he'd been watching
Asian Provocateur. What followed took the gloss right off it.
'Well, I just say that's amazing because you are legend for
me,' I said, in the type of English that would see me fail
the citizenship test. Wrighty was polite, but I could tell
he'd realized he wasn't going to get any decent chat out of
me. Later I messaged my friend Ian Stone, who was doing

a radio show with Wrighty, and asked him to apologize on my behalf. Ian told me that would be super-weird so the circle of cringe was complete.

In America, we'd managed to get Arsenio Hall involved in the show. It was an episode in which Mum got a treat, and her obsession with *Coming to America* meant that Arsenio was an excellent choice. In the show we met him, then went wine tasting together. I have to say, this all felt incredibly surreal. I mean, I went wine tasting with Arsenio Hall and my mum in LA. That's mad, isn't it? We did the day's filming and afterwards we ended up chatting. Flo had flown out to visit me in LA that week, and Arsenio made the classic move of asking her if she was my makeup artist. Flo the super-feminist hid her anger at the assumption and explained she was my agent, at which point Arsenio did such a charming bit about how lovely her accent was that Flo was won over.

Meanwhile he had taken a shine to me and told me he would love to do a gig together where he'd bring me on as his guest. That sounded amazing so, of course, I agreed, not really expecting it to be followed up.

True to his word, though, Arsenio sent me an email with a couple of dates, asking me when would work. We sorted something out, and he told me his assistant would meet me outside the gig, where he was appearing as a surprise guest. Great. I really have no idea where my life would have to get to for me to have an assistant, but I'm always impressed when someone has one. Maybe when my kids grow up I'll give them false names and force them to pick up my takeaways.

The gig was at the Icehouse in Pasadena, and I was driven there by Eric Pankowski, the American executive who had initially asked us to bring a show over to the States. We walked up to the venue and, sure enough, Arsenio's assistant was waiting for us. He took us to the back area of the club and explained that Arsenio would join us later. What was weird, though, was that because I had been brought into the gig by Arsenio, everybody was treating me like royalty. They were all, like, 'Hey, just wanted to say, it's an honour to have one of Arsenio's friends come down.' It was happening so much that I started to become anxious that Arsenio might have built me up a bit too much.

In my head, this was how I hoped it would go: Arsenio goes up, does a bit of chat, talks about how he's met a comedian from the UK and he'd like to bring him on, then I go up to deliver my set, riding the love Arsenio has set up for me. Then he comes on, smashes it, the crowd go wild, he comes off and says he loves me so much he wants me to be in *Coming To America 2*. That was how I saw it going down.

The reality was very different. Arsenio turned up, was very nice and I was informed that he would go up first and do fifteen minutes, then bring me on to do seven or eight. So, unknown brown man was following movie star Arsenio Hall. I'll be honest, that's not the easiest gig for anyone, let alone someone who has zero profile in the US. They announced the surprise guest as Arsenio and the crowd lost their minds. Madness. He went up and started doing bits about being mistaken for other black movie stars – killing it. Talking about exercise – killing it. The whole set killing it. And the whole time he was killing it

I was watching from the back of the room, thinking *I am going to die on my arse here.*

Arsenio finished his set to a STANDING OVATION. He then went to bring me on, clearly forgot my name and just said, 'Next on is a British guy I like!' By this point I was seriously considering doing a runner. And if you want to know how that story goes then wait for *Straight Outta Crawley*, Vol. 2! Just kidding. It went shit.

Acknowledgements

I would love to take the opportunity to thank a few people for what they've done for me, and without whom I would not have been here. I should point out that if I've left anyone out, it's because you do not matter in my life.

To Leesa: I know I wrote a shitty dedication at the front of this book, but I really did mean it. You are a genuine financial pressure. But more than that, without you I would not have been a comedian, or in fact be as happy (?!) as I am. That's right, this is me happy. I took us to the absolute brink, and I really wouldn't blame you if you'd been cheating . . . Have you? If you have, I'd rather you just told me. Is it that bloke you're always chatting to at the gym? The one who you're always playing with your hair when you talk to? Can you just tell me, please? Who am I kidding? You're never going to bloody read this. Anyway, thank you so much for your unflinching support, and being such an incredible wife and mother. I honestly am so lucky to have found someone with such a wonderful heart, an amazing sense of humour, and a complete refusal to watch anything I fucking do.

To the boys, Theo, Alex and Charlie: Thank you so much for being the most wonderful sons anyone could ever ask for. I know I make jokes, but I feel so incredibly lucky that you are my children. You have your own incredible personalities, likes and dislikes, and I don't know why I'm writing that as if it's an amazing thing – you're humans not cats. I worry about you all so much, but at the same time I'm not worried because I've already seen enough to know you're going to be amazing. Thank you for being more like your mum than me. Imagine if you all looked like me – it'd be so difficult for you to have sex. Trust me. Love you, boys.

To Mum: I'm mainly thanking you because if I only thank Leesa and not you you'll never speak to me again, and I think that would be bad – though I wouldn't mind just seeing what that's like for a bit. Thank you for going through what you went through to bring Dinesh and me up single-handedly for a long time. I cannot ever repay you for what you did for us, and nor do I have any intention of doing so. I don't think I've met anyone in my life as strong as you, or as willing to tell somebody when you think they look fat. I love you, Mum, thank you.

To Dinesh: You've been such an incredible younger brother, and I wish I was so much more like you. I look up to you. You're funny, good-looking, slim, and you can look in the same direction with both of your eyes. It really is admirable. Thank you for being there for me, even in the darkest of times, and for being understanding when I wasn't there as much as I should have been. I'm honoured to be able to call you my brother and friend. You've done so much to keep us close and I'll never forget it. In truth, though, I'd forgotten already and only really remembered when writing this bit. But thank you. Love you, bro.

To Flo: Thank you for showing such incredible patience with someone who has the organizational skills of a wounded badger. You were the first person who ever told me you saw real potential in my act. It's very easy to tell someone you want to work with them when they're established, or have been going for a while; it is another thing entirely to support them when they've just ten minutes of material and can't even get regular club work. You did that. So thanks, Flo – it really means a lot. You're the best cuzi. I would say I'd repay you, but you've been getting commission for years now.

To Dad: The other day, I was talking about you to Leesa, and the lights flickered. Was that you? If it wasn't that's annoying because it means both that there might not be an afterlife and also our electrics are shagged. You were such an incredible father, and I wish you'd realized that. I miss you every single day, and I wish you'd been around just a little bit longer, even just to meet our youngest kid. See you soon. Unless there is no afterlife. Flicker the lights again now if there is . . . Shit!

ABOUT THE AUTHOR

Romesh Ranganathan is a stand-up comedian and actor. A former maths teacher, he made his comedy circuit debut in 2010, and has quickly established himself as one of British comedy's brightest stars. His two Edinburgh Festival shows, *Rom Com* and *Rom Wasn't Built In a Day*, were nominated for the prestigious Edinburgh Foster's Best Newcomer Award 2013 and Best Show Award 2014. In 2015 his BBC series *Asian Provocateur* was nominated for a BAFTA and received wide critical acclaim. In 2016 his debut solo tour, *Irrational*, sold over 100,000 tickets and saw Romesh receive the Ents24 Hardest Working Comedian of the Year award.

Romesh appears frequently on multiple TV and radio shows, is the star of *Asian Provocateur*, *The Misadventures of Romesh Ranganathan*, *The Reluctant Landlord* and *Just Another Immigrant*, and a regular on *A League of Their Own*. He writes occasionally for the *Guardian*.